Cognitive Science Series, 2

Cognitive Science Series

Culture and Inference

A Trobriand Case Study

Edwin Hutchins

Harvard University Press
Cambridge, Massachusetts
London, England
1980

Library of Congress Cataloging in Publication Data

Hutchins, Edwin.
  Culture and inference.

  (Cognitive science series ; 2)
  Bibliography: p.
  Includes index.
  1. Ethnology—Papua New Guinea—Trobriand Islands.
2. Cognition and culture—Papua New Guinea—Trobriand
Islands. 3. Land tenure (Primitive law)—Papua New
Guinea—Trobriand Islands. 4. Ethnological jurisprudence.
I. Title. II. Series. [DNLM: 1. Cross-Cultural com-
parison. 2. Culture. 3. Logic.
W1 CO107Th v. 2 / BC199.I47 H974c]
GN671.N5H87   995'.3   80-13280
ISBN 0-674-17970-6

To the memory of
Elaine E. Hutchins

Preface

AS ONE OF THREE graduate assistants, I accompanied Professor Theodore Schwartz to Manus Island in Papua New Guinea in the summer of 1973 to work with the peoples of the south coast of Manus and the islands lying offshore. For three months our daily lives were intertwined with those of the Manus people. Like so many field-workers before me, I was impressed by the intelligence, resourcefulness, and wisdom of the people with whom I lived. Yet there was a striking discontinuity between the work I was doing and the life I was living. Whereas my daily interactions with people told me that they were quite capable of elaborate reasoning strategies, the battery of intelligence tests we administered showed the unschooled village adults to be performing at a level appropriate for an elementary school child in our society. One way to deal with this anomaly is to invoke criticisms of the tests. The tests were, after all, very alien contexts of performance for the New Guinea villager. Even if the tests were somehow unfair, I still could not articulate what it was about my observations of everyday life that led me to find these people intelligent.

Two years later I arrived in another part of Papua New Guinea, this time intending explicitly to document the sort of natural activities in which natives demonstrate their reasoning abilities. This book is a report of a part of that research. This whole endeavor rested on the conviction that a careful analysis of real-world skilled behavior can yield scientific data about the cognitive processes involved in the production of that behavior. The problem was that I had no idea what such a careful analysis ought to look like.

The mode of analysis that emerged here evolved in response to the constraints of my knowledge of what was going on and my knowledge of how to model what was going on. Both of these sets of knowledge are, of course, imperfect. This book is therefore in some sense a testament to my belief that a person's reach should exceed his grasp. I feel strongly that I have overreached my grasp, but if by doing so I can point the way for further work on the study of cognition in natural settings, then I am quite happy to have done so.

The research on which this study is based was conducted in the Trobriand Islands of Papua New Guinea between July 1975 and September 1976. Funding for the field portion of the research, and partial support during the writing, were provided by the Foreign Area Fellowship program (Asia Division) of the Social Science Research Council and American Association of Learned Societies. Partial support while the book was being written was also provided by National Institute of Mental Health grant MH-19864. I am also grateful to Sandra Hutchins and Fay, Helen, and Dan Castile for providing additional financial resources.

In the face of the often trying circumstances of field research, my wife and I received generous assistance from Frank and Jill Holland and Ray Hargraves. We thank them for their help and for their friendship. Our greatest debt is, of course, to the people of the Trobriand Islands, and especially to the people of Tukwaukwa village, who shared their lives with us for a year.

Since the work presented here is an attempted synthesis of several fields, my intellectual debts are many and diverse. The ethnographic description of land tenure presented in chapter 2 benefited from conversations (both in the U.S. and in the Trobriands) with Annette Weiner. I am grateful to Theodore Schwartz for his professional guidance and his friendship over the past ten years. I thank him for introducing me simultaneously to fieldwork and to Melanesia. Roy D'Andrade started me thinking about culture and inference and provided much needed advice. I owe Michael Cole special thanks for encouraging me to publish this work. I thank Christopher Riesbeck and Geoffrey Hinton for their careful reading of the manuscript and for introducing me to artificial intelligence in a serious way. Others who provided help and inspiration were Donald Norman, David Rumelhart, Donald Tuzin, Naomi Quinn, Paul Kay, Aaron Cicourel, and James Levin. Finally, I want to express my gratitude to my wife, Dona, who made valuable contributions to every aspect of this research. Without her assistance in documenting the Trobriand language in the field and at home, this project would never have reached completion.

Contents

Culture and Inference

1 | Introduction

PERHAPS THE OLDEST and most fundamental question in anthropology is, in what ways are all people the same and in what ways do they differ? The differences of opinion on this have been nowhere greater than in the portion of the field concerned with modes of human thought. Historically, the forces that shaped opinion on this topic have included the economics and politics of imperialism as well as scientific evidence. Over the years a number of positions have shown themselves to be quite robust. Anthropologists have variously asserted an evolutionary position that distinguishes civilized from primitive thought in terms of developmental criteria, a relativist position of separate but equal modes of thought, and a psychic unity position in which all of mankind is loaded into the same psychological basket.

The observable manifestations of human thought are incredibly varied and the relation of thought to its observable manifestations appears to be very complex. In the absence of an explicit theory of what thought is and how it is related to observable phenomena, each of these positions can be "demonstrated" by making certain (usually sub-rosa) assumptions and choosing appropriate observations. This book is an attempt to explore the nature of reasoning in a so-called "primitive" society via a theory that has been developing over the past twenty or so years in the intersection of the fields that are now calling themselves parts of cognitive science. Since this book stands at the convergence of a number of lines of thought, I would like, by way of introduction, to trace some of those lines briefly.

Background

In the middle 1950s a "need to be explicit about internal symbolic mechanisms" (Newell and Simon, 1972, p. 4) was recognized by some anthropologists, psychologists, and linguists. This realization resulted from the development in World War II of cybernetics and control theory and the postwar development of computer science. Together these advances provided the conceptual base for imagining operational systems of complex symbolic processes.

This realization brought a change in the research goals of some members of each of these fields, such that descriptions of the observed regularities in behavior were augmented with descriptions of possible internal symbolic mechanisms which were capable of producing the regularities of behavior observed. In anthropology this shift was a move away from the notion of culture as what people do and toward a notion of culture as what people have to know in order to do what they do. Parallel developments appeared in linguistics as the theory of transformational grammar and in psychology as a new interest in previously frowned-upon mentalism (Newell and Shaw, 1957; Miller, 1956; Miller, Galanter, and Pribram, 1960). The research strategies of these approaches involved the construction of models of cognitive organization which were judged virtuous or not in terms of their ability to produce or predict behavior similar to that of humans performing a given task.

The proposed isomorphism between behavior of man and behavior of model was, of course, fairly strongly hedged by saying that the model produces some aspect of the behavior of the human task performer, for clearly no model will be complex enough to account for the entire range of a person's behavior. The organization of the model itself was to be governed by the nature of the task and the aspect of the task performer's behavior to be accounted for. In the early explorations, however, the organization of the model was as often determined by the nature of the analytic techniques borrowed from other applications and disciplines as it was by the actual behavior to be accounted for.[1]

Early on in the anthropological shift there was theoretical interest in the possibility of discovering internal symbolic mechanisms that could act as a sort of grammar of a culture. In 1964 Paul Kay, building on Goodenough's (1957) notion of a description of culture as a sort of grammar, read a paper to the American Anthropological Association meetings in which he said, "Culture bears much the same relation to social behavior as does language to speech behavior. Both are codes that describe *some aspects* of all the relevant behaviors but all the aspects of no particular behaviors. A theory of culture, like a grammar—which is a theory of language—has two major functions. First, it distinguishes hypothetical behaviors that are possible according to the standards of the community from those that are impossible by these standards" (Kay, 1966, p. 106).

The second major function of a theory of culture is "to give some structural account of the behaviors it allows. In the case of grammar, the largest units of behavior of which a structural account is given are usually sentences. A comparably solid unit has not yet been established for culture, but the present work . . . suggests that the proposition may turn out to be the appropriate unit" (p. 108).

Taking culture to be an interconnected set of propositions, Kay isolated several problems to be solved. Among them were the discovery of a set of propositions that are implicitly embodied in natural utterances and the discovery of the relations that are believed to obtain among such propositions: "We are looking here for a structure which is immanent but not necessarily explicit in native discourse—a structure that plays in native discourse the role that logic plays in scientific discourse. Such a structure includes as parts (a) certain axiom-like analytic statements that rarely if ever appear in ordinary discourse . . . and (b) the rules of inference of the native belief system—e.g., modus ponens, if the informant is a Western philosopher" (p. 109).

Unfortunately, no empirical research pursued these interests in the years immediately following. In large part this was due to there being available no tools that seemed appropriate to the discovery of such structures.

Classification

In anthropology the first major wave of research to focus on explicit representation of internal symbolic mechanisms was the investigation of systems of classification or categorization. Given the acuity of the human senses, the world of experience contains "an infinite number of perceptably different things" (Rosch, 1974, p. 177). But no organism treats every event and object as a unique entity. Experience is cut up into categories by which similar, but nonidentical, stimuli can be seen as instances of the same thing. Borrowing the concept of distinctive features from linguistics, anthropologists began searching for the distinctive semantic features which could be used to distinguish terms in lexical domains. In a componential analysis, distinctive features were used both to signify the necessary and sufficient conditions for determining the class of objects a term referred to, thereby defining the terms, and also to signify the conditions by which the terms could be distinguished from and contrasted with each other.[2] The distinctive features were thought to be those which had to be attended to by the individual in order to map the potentially infinite universe of experience onto a finite universe of "culturally defined and linguistically labeled categories" (Frake, 1961, p. 115). The categories were

then the constituents of an internal symbolic representation of experience, and the classification models were supposed to account
for the individual's ability to identify and label events and objects
as instances of category members.

Thus, an important part of the knowledge people must have in
order to do what they do is knowledge of how to categorize experience. While the nature of the process by which classification is accomplished is still at issue, the impact of culture upon classification
is now well documented.[3]

In response to what might be characterized as the selective pres-
sure of the information processing approach, there have been several major departures from the distinctive-feature/componential-
analysis format. First, it was noted that while distinctive-feature
models were elegant and in some formal sense very satisfying, the
degree to which they could be said to account for any aspect of
people's actual processing on a particular task was problematic.
When several different models of the mental structure said to
underlie labeling behavior in a particular semantic domain all predict that behavior equally well, how does a researcher know which
one, if any, the informant is actually using? This question of the
psychological reality of the models was most forcefully posed by
Burling (1964). Attempts to answer it led to the realization that if a
model was to account for the output of an information processing
routine, it could not do so by reference to the organization of the
representation alone. A sufficient model needs also to specify how
the representation is used—how people go about knowing whatever
it is they know (Wallace, 1965; D'Andrade, 1976).

A second problem with componential analysis was that while it
worked reasonably well for some domains (for example, kinship
and reference pronouns), for other domains (illness is a notable
early example) attempts at componential analysis consistently produced unsatisfactory results.[4] There was apparently no simple set
of distinctive features for defining categories in many domains.
Other techniques were required to discover the semantic organization of these domains.

One of these other techniques involved the consideration of non-
criterial as well as criterial attributes. D'Andrade, Quinn, Nerlove,
and Romney (1972) used a measure of distributional similarity to
assess the salience of diseases and their properties. A list of diseases
and relevant properties was compiled from interviews with informants and from the researchers' own beliefs about diseases. Each
property was then rewritten in a sentence frame format, for example, "you can catch _____ from other people" (cf. Frake,
1964; Metzger and Williams, 1963). All combinations of sentence

frames and diseases were presented to informants, who judged each combination to be either true or false.[5] The resulting matrix of disease by property co-occurrences was then analyzed using factor analysis, hierarchical clustering, and multidimensional scaling. When applied to a co-occurrence matrix of thirty diseases by thirty properties, all three techniques gave convergent results, indicating that the structure obtained was not technique-specific.

D'Andrade and colleagues drew three major conclusions from their study. First, that the defining properties of a set of terms are not always the properties which determine how people categorize or react to these terms. Second, that the model of lexical domains as organized into taxonomic and paradigmatic relations is not always useful. Third, that neither the large data matrices elicited from informants nor the spatial arrays of the multidimensional scaling solution were satisfactory representations of the knowledge base used by informants. The former was unwieldy and lacked generative capacity while the latter threw out information about specific relations. Yet the informants had been able to answer the hundreds of questions represented in the matrices. Looking ahead, the authors said,

> Perhaps a belief system may be represented as a set of propositions, capable of generating such data matrices (Kay 1966). At present we have little empirical evidence about the form of such propositions; our initial inclination is to use the symbolic apparatus of logic, especially first order predicate logic, which remains relatively close to a natural language format. In any case, whatever form these propositions eventually take, the problem will be to develop decision procedures which can economically generate assessments of "truth" and "likelihood" which are the same as those made by informants. (D'Andrade, Quinn, Nerlove, and Romney, 1972, pp. 52-53)

Following up on these conclusions, D'Andrade (1976) attempted to construct a propositional model for the American beliefs about illness. He wondered if a set of propositions capable of generating the matrix could be extracted from the matrix data itself. The informants in the original study had attributed each property to a set of diseases. D'Andrade asked of every pair of properties in the data matrix, "Is the set of diseases having one of these properties a subset of the set of diseases having the other?" To do that, a two-by-two contingency table was constructed for every pair of properties (see Fig. 1). With the exception of appendicitis, every disease which has the property of bringing on fever also has the property of being caused by germs. The class of diseases which bring on fever is a subset of the class of diseases which are caused by germs. This situ-

Brings on fever

	yes	no
Is caused by germs — yes	whooping cough typhoid fever tonsilitis strep throat small pox pneumonia mumps mononucleosis measles malaria laryngitis influenza a cold chicken pox bronchitis	tuberculosis syphilis polio gonorrhea
Is caused by germs — no	appendicitis	cancer dental cavities epilepsy heart attack leukemia poison ivy psychosis rheumatism stroke ulcers

Figure 1.   *A binary contingency chart (D'Andrade, 1976)*

ation can be represented by a proposition of the form "If a disease brings on fever, then it is caused by germs." Notice that the proposition is not about relations among particular diseases but among classes of diseases which are defined by the presence or absence of particular properties. Reworking the entire analysis in this way, and relying on the transitivity of the subset relations (that is, if A is a subset of B and B is a subset of C, then A is a subset of C), D'Andrade was able to represent the knowledge about the relations between 30 diseases and 27 properties as a set of propositions with about one-fifth the information storage required by the matrix itself. The ability of the propositional representation to produce the larger matrix is a demonstration of its generative capacity. In addition to having a generative capacity, the propositional model, unlike the multidimensional scaling, saved information, such as the relation of germs to contagion, which seemed to encode underlying cultural understandings of *how* the world works.

In responding to the need to be careful about the specification of *how* people go about believing *what* they believe, D'Andrade changed the organization of the representation. It is important to see that in so doing, he also changed the aspect of behavior which his model accounts for. Classification models answer the question, "What is it?" The propositional model here answers the question, "If I know a given disease has property X, what other properties do I know it has?" The model can do this because it contains not only information about the relations of terms to their defining properties but information about the relations among the properties themselves. In D'Andrade's illness model, these relations are subset/superset relations, but, as he points out, many other kinds of relations may in fact hold among the properties.

A variety of kinds of symbolic relations have already been investigated by anthropologists (Frake, 1964; Metzger and Williams, 1963 and 1966; Atkins and Curtis, 1969; Triandis, 1972). Casagrande and Hale (1967) list 13 relations which are found to connect concepts in Papago folk definitions. The list includes: membership, subset/superset, order (precedence), attributive, part whole, contingency, co-occurrence, cause, equivalence, source, and analogy. The important thing about these relations is that they all permit certain inferences. Some, such as subset/superset, carry inferences very generally, while others (for example, source) support inference only in limited contexts. It is the presence of relations that do support inference which provides for the generative capacity of any semantic structure. As Collins and Quillian (1972, p. 324) point out, "The relations that carry inferences always form the basis for organizing any semantic information or subject matter . . . It is by using inference that people can know much more than they learn."

A model with a generative capacity is an important step closer than categorization models to the sort of cultural grammar that was originally hoped for. One of the major complaints about classification models is that the aspects of behavior they account for, while clearly essential to cognition, have not often been shown to be directly related to the sorts of behaviors in which most social scientists are interested. In *Pigs for the Ancestors* (1968) Roy Rappaport notes that it is "the cognized model of the functional relationships among the entities which people think are part of their environment" that guides an actor's actions. But in a footnote, he observes,

The method of ethnoscience pioneered by Conklin (1959) and Frake (1962) and others, while valuable, has largely been directed toward the elucidation of native taxonomic distinctions, and taxonomic distinctions do not necessarily indicate folk notions of functional process. The exploration of functional relationships still rests, it seems to me, on the rather impressionistic methods that have prevailed in anthropology, although it may be that a structural approach similar to that advocated by Claude Lévi-Strauss and Edmund Leach or the "cultural grammars" suggested by some other writers could be of use. (p. 238)

If we are to build a model of functional knowledge, however, more than the relations among the terms of the representation must change. In the ethnoscience model, the world of the perceiver was divided into discrete lexical domains which had clear boundaries. In a model of functional knowledge, on the other hand, an instance of a concept from one domain may have relations—functional and otherwise—to concepts from many other domains. Frake (1964) notes an important implication of this: "If a semantic domain is a set of related concepts, then it is clear that there is no one way to separate the conceptual structure of the people into a finite number of discrete, clearly delimited domains. Rather, we have a network of relations whose links enable us to travel along a variety of paths from one concept to another" (p. 141). A domain of discourse, then, is not a clearly bounded set of propositions in the way that a lexical domain is a clearly bounded set of lexemes.

The increasing interest in the processes involved in people's using their knowledge brought a reorganization of the representation of what people know. It was clear to many workers in the field that a propositional representation with a set of inference procedures which could operate on the representation was probably a better model of the cognition involved in many natural tasks than a componential analysis, a taxonomy, or a multidimensional scaling. Abelson and Carroll (1965), Colby (1964, 1967), and others in cognitive psychology and artificial intelligence constructed simple propositional models of individual belief systems which supported this position. But for the anthropologists, several problems stood in the way of directly developing such a model.

Perhaps the major stumbling block here concerns the nature of inferential processes. The studies cited above assume that certain types of inference underlie the ability of Americans to make a large number of statements on the basis of a small, richly interconnected network of belief. But what effect would cross-cultural differences in modes of inference making (if they existed) have on the processing of such representations?

Inference

There is a tradition of research on the nature of the reasoning abilities of nonliterate peoples that uses verbal logic problems as the primary research tool. In the 1930s A. R. Luria (1976), a student of L. S. Vygotsky, collected data on syllogistic reasoning from collectivized and noncollectivized Central Asian peasants. Luria used two types of verbal syllogisms. In one type, the content of the problem was taken from the everyday experience of the peasants; in the other, the content was unrelated to their everyday experience. All of the subjects performed adequately on the syllogisms concerning everyday life, but on those syllogisms that did not concern everyday experience, the schooled peasants, or those engaged in collective planning, performed much better than the unschooled peasants. When dealing with familiar materials, the unschooled subjects characteristically supported their answers by appealing to the facts of experience. In dealing with the unfamiliar materials, they "refused to accept the system of logical assumptions and to draw conclusions from them" (Cole and Scribner, 1974, p. 161).

Consider the following example from Luria's work. Presented with the premises, "In the far north all bears are white; Novaya Zemyla is in the far north. What color are the bears there?" peasant women would often answer, "I don't know. You should ask the people who have been there and seen them." This is a response that clearly fails the task presented to the subject.

Subsequent research by Cole, Gay, Glick, and Sharp (1971) shows a similar pattern for Liberian Kpelle subjects. Unschooled subjects attempt "to handle the problem on a factual basis" (p. 162). They often reject the experimenter-given premises of the problem and substitute more socially appropriate premises in their place. Following up on this finding, Scribner designed a task in which the subject was asked to repeat the premises of the problem back to the experimenter twice—once after having heard and attempted to solve the problem and then again immediately after being read the problem for a second time. This procedure yielded the startling result that while the first recall contained transformations of the sort described above, "the second recall, given immediately after the subject reheard the problem, was often no more complete nor accurate than the first" (Cole and Scribner, 1974, p. 165). Rather than simply conclude that the subjects had failed the task outright, Scribner took it upon herself to try to understand what the subject was doing. In looking more closely at the protocols, she discovered that wherever there was sufficient information to reconstruct the chain of reasoning leading to the answer, it was found to follow logically from the evidence used by the subject.

We can imagine the premises and the chain of reasoning which led to the answer about the bears in Novaya Zemyla above. Assume for the sake of argument that the subject believed (1) that in order to know the color of something one would have to see it, and (2) in order to see something one would have to be in physical proximity with it. With these quite reasonable premises the subject could reason that since she was not in physical proximity to the place, she could not have seen the bear there; and if she did not see the bear, she could not know what color it was. This chain of reasoning involves two instances of what is called *modus tollendo tollens* reasoning (reasoning from the consequent). This inference is generally regarded as being more difficult than the *modus ponens* (reasoning from the antecedent) that the "correct" solution to the problem required. If this is the case, and it seems quite possible that it is, then in the course of producing a response that *fails* the task, the subject has performed a feat of reasoning much more difficult than that required by a successful solution.

The work of Mary Henle (1962) with American college students and that of Wason and Johnson-Laird (1972) with British university students indicates that the same verbal reasoning strategies are prevalent among the members of industrialized societies as well. Henle presented subjects with syllogistic tasks embedded in simple interpersonal scenarios. When asked to justify apparently fallacious inferences made in response to the tasks, Henle's subjects often altered the premises given by the problem, omitted premises, or added their own premises. The inferences the subjects made followed by the conventional rules of logic from the premises they assumed, but the premises they assumed were often not those given by the problem.

The experiments performed by Wason and Johnson-Laird provide a comparison between performances on two formally equivalent reasoning tasks. Both problems involve concepts which are familiar to the subjects. One is a task to be performed with two-sided paper labels, and the other a task to be performed with letter envelopes. In each case the subjects are given a rule—in the form of a conditional statement—which specifies allowable combinations of concept values. In the label task, the rule is, "If a label has a vowel on one side, then it has an even number on the other." In the letter task, the rule is, "If a letter envelope is sealed, then it has a five-penny stamp on it." Subjects in each task are shown items one side at a time and are asked to indicate which items would have to be turned over to be sure the rule has not been violated. The subjects performed consistently better on the letter task than on the label task in spite of the fact that the tasks have the same formal structure. On the label task even university students achieved only about a five percent success rate, while on the envelope task their success rate was around seventy percent. The difference between the performances on the task cannot be attributed to differential familiarity with the concepts involved, since university students should be expected to be as familiar with even numbers and vowel characters as they are with stamps and sealed envelopes. The difference is that the letter problem is easily represented in terms of prior cultural knowledge about the relation between postal rates and the sealing of envelopes, while there is no corresponding cultural knowledge about the relation of letters to numbers on opposite sides of labels whose use is unknown. It appears that the performance of inference is not enabled by meaningful conceptual content alone, but by familiar conceptual content organized in culturally meaningful ways.

In the initial design of each of these experiments the representation of the problem was assumed to be given by the task. The investigator's job was to specify an appropriate classical reasoning solution and then to observe the performance to see whether or not it mirrored the "correct" result. The difficulty encountered in each of these experiments is that we seem not to be justified in assuming that the representation of the problem is necessarily given by the premises of the task. Cultural knowledge is clearly involved in the subject's comprehension of the task content and the task requirements. Instead of measuring reasoning abilities, these tasks seem to measure the subject's ability to interpret the meaning of the premises of the problem. If the premises of the problem lack cultural meaning (due either to the inappropriateness of the concepts related or to the relation posited by the problem between the concepts), then the subject—be he university student or illiterate rice farmer—is unlikely to arrive at the solution deemed by the experimenter to be logically correct. In light of their experience in Africa, Cole and Scribner (1974) conclude, "It is quite clear that we cannot draw conclusions about reasoning processes from the *answers* people give to logic problems. We have first to ask, 'What is their understanding of the task? How do they encode the information presented to them? What transformation does the information undergo, and what factors control these?' " (p. 166).

It seems that the search for representations of what people know, as exemplified by the ethnoscience tradition in anthropology, got into trouble largely because it ignored the processes of how people go about knowing. On the other hand, the search for characterizations of how people make inferences has suffered from a failure to consider what it is that people are thinking about. Surely this results because representation and process, while analytically separable, are intimately intertwined in any real instance of cognition. They are two sides of the same mental coin. Given the traditional boundaries of the academic disciplines, it is easy to see why anthropologists would like to study cultural beliefs without having to worry about psychological processes and why psychologists would like to study cognitive processes without reference to specific cultural beliefs. But to do either of these is to miss much of what cognition is about. The fact that the study of either representation or process really does require the study of the other is one of the best reasons I can think of for taking an interdisciplinary approach.

A Naturalistic Approach

Under what conditions can we observe an individual's performance on an information processing task and still have some way to constrain conjectures about how the individual represents the information being processed? One possibility is to turn the subject's tendency to interpret the problem in terms of his own cultural grammar to our advantage by observing an information processing task in its natural (cultural) context. Given the problems observed in the reasoning experiments described above, the researcher might achieve better "control" of the experiment if he tried to discover how the subject represents his own natural task rather than trying to teach the subject a way to represent an artificial task. Cole and colleagues (1971) considered such an approach to Kpelle litigation. They note, "Because it is public, explicit, and relatively formal, and because debating is valued by the Kpelle, the law case offers one promising natural setting in which to observe individuals as they construct arguments and draw conclusions from data" (p. 178). They present a brief excerpt from a Kpelle divorce case, but do not analyze it, noting that they do not have the knowledge required to determine how the participants are using what they know. But the knowledge that is required is at once both the cultural grammar that we are looking for and the sort of understanding that a good traditional ethnographer is supposed to acquire in his fieldwork.

Obviously, it is not quite that simple, or we would not still be waiting for someone to produce a cultural grammar. A major difficulty here is that the cultural grammar we are looking for is most often transparent to those who use it. Once learned, it becomes what one *sees with,* but seldom what one *sees.* In Kay's comments it is the semantic structure which is "immanent but not explicit in native discourse." This referential transparency of the cultural grammar, which will be shown later to be one of its essential properties, manifests itself in an insidious way in anthropological fieldwork. In an excellent paper on making sense out of statements in Thai discourse, Moerman (1969) points out that coming to think like a native is to some extent required by fieldwork, but it should not be the goal of fieldwork. "It is perhaps charmingly naive for the discipline which prides itself on having realized that it would not be a fish who discovered water to assume that cultural immersion (the longer the better; one just soaks it up) produces scientific knowledge" (p. 450).

The ethnographer ends up internalizing the cultural grammar as he does the grammar of the language, and he uses the cultural grammar to understand (in the highly valued emic sense) the events he observes. He may, however, end up being no more able than an introspective native to specify the nature of the representation and the process which enable him to understand. Moerman, somewhat cynically, says that the moral of his paper is that "while a little knowledge may be dangerous, a great deal of knowledge can be devastating" (p. 449). The moral I draw is not that the ethnographer should avoid learning as much as is possible about the culture in which he immerses himself, but that with a little care, the ethnographer's finest tool—his ability as a human being to learn another's culture—can be used to produce scientific knowledge. To do so, however, the ethnographer must make some attempt to discover and *explicitly represent* the knowledge structure on which understandings are based. A major impediment to this exercise has been the relative scarcity in anthropology of examples of explicit representations of functional knowledge which are compelling in their ability to explain phenomena of interest to anthropologists.

It seems to me that there is another important convergence of interests in cognitive science here. While these other lines of research were being pursued in anthropology and cross-cultural psychology, cognitive psychologists and researchers in artificial intelligence were trying to develop models of the cognition involved in a number of everyday tasks. Major advances were made here in the areas of language understanding in general (Winograd, 1972; Schank, 1972) and story understanding in particular (Charniak, 1972; Rumelhart, 1975). Two of the major findings of this line of work are directly applicable to the sort of problem sketched here. They are (1) that the comprehension of a piece of connected discourse requires some sort of knowledge structure onto which the language can be mapped, and (2) that in the course of understanding, many inferences are made; that is, people understand facts about the story that are not explicitly in the text of the story itself. On this view, inference is not a special cognitive ability reserved for special effortful situations, but is rather an integral part of our continual and seemingly effortless understanding of the everyday world.

All of these projects share the common goal of developing models which meet what Newell and Simon (1972) call the sufficiency criterion. The idea is that a model is a theory of the task, and when properly developed, "the theory performs the task it explains" (p. 10).

From an anthropological point of view, the virtue of the artificial intelligence methodology is that nothing can be taken for granted.

If one is trying to explicitly model the processing of a person doing an everyday task, then every bit of knowledge required by the task must be made explicit. The computer knows nothing that it is not in some sense told. The artificial intelligence methodology forces the modeler to be explicit about the sorts of knowledge and understanding that are normally implicitly assumed in our everyday dealing with the world. If he fails to explicitly represent some underlying assumption, no matter how trivial or mundane, his simulations generate nonsense. Sometimes that nonsense can be very entertaining, but the point of generating the nonsense in the first place is that the modeler can compare the interpretations his program makes with his own interpretations and the difference between them can help him discover things that went into his own interpretation that he was never before aware of. Once he has discovered these, he has a chance to incorporate them in his model. It is in this sense that the artificial intelligence methodology can contribute to the solution of one of the anthropologist's major problems, the referential transparency of cultural beliefs.

Traditional anthropological method offers a partial analogue of the artificial intelligence discovery technique. It consists of putting oneself into an alien culture and trying to notice differences between the interpretations one makes and those made by the natives. Such observations can provide valuable information about the unspoken assumptions of the other culture, but, as was noted above, it is also possible to assimilate such assumptions without ever being explicitly aware of having done so.

The artificial intelligence methodology seems to offer at least partial solutions to many of the problems outlined in this chapter. It is an approach in which representation and process are considered together and it forces explicit representation of the phenomena of interest. It is of course not without its problems. A problem which is of concern here is that once one has constructed a model, it may be difficult to assess the goodness of fit between the performance of the model and the performance of the system being modeled. The difficulty of this depends upon the nature of the process being modeled. When the processes are easily captured in experimental situations, the performance of a simulation can be compared directly with the performance of subjects in experimental situations. When the processes concern naturalistic phenomena, the assessment of goodness of fit is much more difficult.

Organization of the Argument

The domain of discourse for which a cultural code will be presented is public land litigation in the Trobriand Islands of Papua New Guinea. The Trobriands are a group of tropical coral islands lying in the Solomon Sea about 120 miles north of the extreme eastern tip of the New Guinea mainland. The 13,000 people of these islands rely primarily on subsistence agriculture for their livelihood. Land is of utmost importance in the Trobriands because all wealth and power is ultimately rooted in land. Land litigation was chosen as the domain to model because the data are easily accessible and because it involves conceptual structures that are central to Trobriand social life and so are likely to be widely shared by members of the society. It was also chosen because it contains active reasoning. People involved in it have to think on their feet, as it were, and their accounts of their own reasoning in such circumstances are richer than is the case in other domains of discourse such as narrative, where the demands on reasoning are not so rigorous.

I shall attempt to demonstrate by example how such an integrative approach can be applied to the question of the nature of reasoning. The argument proceeds by the following steps:

Chapter 2 presents a more or less traditional ethnographic account of the relations between people and land in the Trobriand Islands. Special attention is given here to the lexicon of rights in land and a small class of exchange activities that are essential to the transfer of rights in land. This chapter is a description of what is possible and what is impossible in the arena of land rights from the Trobriand point of view.

Chapter 3 takes up the question of the extent to which an investigator is justified in making inferences about the nature of someone else's inferences on the basis of an examination of natural discourse. This issue is complicated in this case by the fact that the discourse is foreign to virtually every reader. Sorting out what translation is really about points to the necessity of an explicit representation of the logical relations which underlie the logical connectives of discourse. That representation, the model of the cultural code, is provided by a formal notation for the salient concepts and relations among concepts in this domain.

In Chapter 4 the formal notation is applied to segments of discourse taken from an actual case of land litigation. It is shown that the inferences made by the model are those made by the participants to the litigation.

In Chapter 5 the emphasis shifts from the adequacy of the cultural code as a model of folk understanding to the properties such a system displays in use. The participation of the cultural code in a number of higher level cognitive functions (for example, problem solving, decision making, and planning) is demonstrated with examples from the analysis of litigation.

Chapter 6 presents the conclusions of the study with respect to the substantive question of the nature of Trobriand reason and with respect to the methodological issues surrounding the study of cognitive process in natural settings.

2 | Trobriand Land Tenure

MALINOWSKI'S *Coral Gardens and Their Magic* (1965), a two-volume work on agriculture in the Trobriands, is, and will for some time undoubtedly remain, the definitive work on Trobriand Island land tenure. Malinowski described his method of researching land tenure as follows: "The maxim that you cannot understand the rules of the game without a knowledge of the game itself describes the essence of this method. You must know first how man uses his soil, how he weaves round it his traditional legends, his beliefs and mystical values, how he fights for it and defends it; then and then only will you be able to grasp the system of legal and customary rights which define the relationship between man and soil" (vol. 1, p. 320).

Malinowski gave a thorough account of the uses of land and how it was tied up in myth and tradition, but when it came to describing how people actually acquire and defend rights in land he left us guessing. One goal of this book is to fill in the resultant ethnographic gap by describing in some detail how people fight for and defend claims in land. As Malinowski could have predicted, however, considering that sort of data (that "part of the game") forces some changes in our understanding of the "rules of the game." In this chapter I will attempt to develop an ethnographic description of land tenure in the Trobriand Islands which contains the major conceptual relations addressed by litigants in actual instances of land litigation. In doing so I will also refer to two other descriptions of Trobriand land tenure, Powell (1956) and Weiner (1976).

The intended use of an ethnographic description as well as the data considered while assembling it obviously has a considerable influence upon a description's organization and content. For example, Malinowski's description of land tenure, which is best elaborated in the final two chapters of volume one of *Coral Gar-*

dens and Their Magic, was an attempt to explain land tenure in
Kiriwina (the major district of the Trobriand group) as part of a
wider functionally integrated set of institutions. As such it asks and
answers questions such as, "Why are residence units composed as
they are?" and "How does rank operate as a principle of territorial
occupation?" The present chapter hopes to answer quite a different
question, "What does the individual Trobriander have to know in
order to perform adequately in the arena of land litigation?"[1] The
answer to Malinowski's questions are not answers to the question
posed here, but in the course of answering his own questions, Malinowski collected and published a good deal of data relevant to the
present question.

Malinowski proposed four doctrines which "underlie all claims
and control all practices referring to land" (vol. 1, p. 335). Each
doctrine contains a mixture of constraints, some inside and some
outside the awareness of the individual Trobriander himself. As
Malinowski notes, "These four doctrines are not, of course, codi-
fied in any explicit native tradition" (vol. 1, p. 337). In spite of
Malinowski's claims about native psychology, a functional description of the operation of a social system is *not* a description of an
actor's understandings of the system. A complete description,
however, should include both a specification of the actor's understandings of the system, and a description of the behavior of the
system as a whole. The two levels of description are complementary
in that a fuller specification of the actor's understandings should
contribute to our comprehension of the behavior of individuals and
thus to our understanding of the behavior of the system as a whole.

Like Malinowski, Powell (1956) was interested in social dynamics
more than in individual cognition. He reports nothing of land litigation, although he does provide us with quantitative data on the
kin links across which rights to land pass. Weiner (1976) gives brief
reports of two disputes over land and not only traces the movement
of rights in land from individual to individual but describes the set
of principles that make that movement culturally appropriate. The
cases Weiner describes are of a different nature from the cases to be
described here (how they are different will be discussed later) and
only a few sentences of litigation are reported, but the approach
taken here is certainly similar in spirit to that taken by Weiner. I
want to take it one step further, however, and ask how people use
their knowledge to organize their claims to land. The description
that will be presented here should be taken, therefore, as a supple-
ment to, rather than a replacement for, the already existing descriptions.

Relations between Men and Land

While the perspective I assume is not that chosen by any previous ethnographer of Kiriwina, I agree with Malinowski that a description of land tenure is "a coherent story about the relations of the Trobriander to his soil" (1965, vol. 1, p. 321). This will not be a description of the relation of the Trobriander to the produce of his soil, for that is quite a different story. I refer the reader interested in the disbursement of the garden produce to Malinowski's detailed descriptions (vol. 1, pp. 188f). Let me begin the account of land tenure, then, with a description of the units of land to which people bear relations and the cycle of garden work in which those relations are exercised.

A typical Trobriand village as seen from the air appears as two rough concentric circles of houses arranged around a central clearing. Outside the circle of houses is a grove of large fruit bearing trees and stands of coconut and areca (betel nut) palms. Further still from the center of the village are the surrounding garden lands (see Fig. 2). Coconut palm lined footpaths radiate from the village and cut through the garden lands on their way to neighboring settlements. A careful observer in an airplane will notice that the garden lands are divided into large fields. Depending upon the season of one's flight, one might see large areas blackened by recent fires. The fields currently under cultivation appear well organized and free of ground-covering weeds. Others, having been gardened within the last few years, now lie fallow with a light overgrowth of shrubs and small trees. Still others which have not been gardened for many years support stands of large trees and dense undergrowth.

Every gardening community (village or village cluster) has in its vicinity a minimum of from six to seven major gardening fields, *kwabila*. Some large villages have many more than that.[2] In each yearly gardening season, every gardening community must slash, burn, and fence in an area of garden land sufficient to provide every household in the community with its gardening needs. The biggest single job in preparing a *kwabila* for gardening is the construction of a fence around the entire perimeter of the field. This is required to prevent pigs from entering the garden and uprooting the crops. Even if all the pigs in villages were contained, the fences would still be necessary to keep the bush boars out. The work of fencing is undertaken by large cooperative work groups.

The normal fallow period is from five to seven years with a more or less regular rotation among the *kwabila*. The choice of which

Figure 2. *Aerial view of a typical Trobriand village*

kwabila to garden in a particular season depends upon many factors. Primary among them is the fallow time that has elapsed since the last gardening for each *kwabila*. Those fields that have been recently gardened will not be ready for several years. Of those which have lain fallow for sufficient time, some may be preferable to others on the basis of the characteristics of the soil and drainage. It is important that the characteristics of the garden are appropriate for the weather encountered during the gardening, but I do not know to what extent Trobrianders base their choice of a *kwabila* on predictions of the weather in the upcoming season. The choice also depends upon the immediate political plans of the village community. If a gardening competition seems likely, better fields may be taken out of turn. Each year, one or more *kwabila* (depending upon their sizes) will be chosen for the year's gardening by the community.

Every *kwabila* is divided into numerous individual garden plots called *baleku*. As Malinowski points out, "The division of cultivable land and economically appropriated land into *kwabila* and *baleku* is permanent; the boundaries of the *kwabila*, 'large portions' or 'fields' are called *karege'i*, and of the *baleku*, 'small plots,' *tukulumwala*. Such boundaries are indicated by long stone heaps and other landmarks, which remain in position while the soil lies fallow. Economically, each *kwabila* is apportioned to one community, and each community owns a number of *kwabila* surrounding it" (1965, vol. 2, p. 83).

It is in reference to particular *kwabila* and *baleku* that people make claims about their relations to land. Three legal relations between men and land are conceptually and linguistically distinguished by the Trobrianders themselves in the course of reasoning about land: ownership, use rights, and allocation rights.

Ownership

In the Trobriand cosmology, all of mankind is divided among four major exogamous totemic clans, *kumila*. Each major clan is subdivided into a variable number of matrilineal descent groups, *dala* (Malinowski called them subclans) which are ranked relative to each other. The highest ranking are the few *dala* of high chiefs, *guyau;* next are the several *dala* of low chiefs, *gumgweguya;* and lowest are the many *dala* of commoners, *tokai*. An important component of an individual's social identity derives from *dala* membership.

Every parcel of land, be it garden field *kwabila*, house plot *tumila*, domestic grove *weka*, or tract of uncut forest *odila*, is uniquely associated with a particular matrilineal descent group *dala*. A

dala's claim to land is based on a mythological charter which re-
counts how matrilineal ancestors came to be associated with the
lands.[3] Each individual has, by virtue of membership in a *dala,*
a relationship to all lands associated with his or her *dala.* This relationship is designated in the Trobriand language primarily by
the term *tolipwaipwaiya,* composed of the instrumental prefix
toli-, which designates a relation of social responsibility, and the
root *pwaipwaiya,* the generic for "land."[4] This relationship can
also be indicated by the use of the distal forms of possession especially in the plural; thus, *si pwaipwaiya,* "their land," *da pwai-
pwaiyasi,* "our (inclusive plural) land."[5] Those people who are
tolipwaipwaiya to a particular piece of land are referred to by Malinowski and Powell as the "owners" of the land and again by Malinowski as "citizens" of the village to which the land attaches.
Malinowski distinguishes "citizens" from "resident aliens" who
reside in the village without bearing the *tolipwaipwaiya* relation to
any of the lands gardened by the village. In a loose sense we can
consider the *tolipwaipwaiya* to be "owners" of land, yet the *tolipwaipwaiya* relation by itself does not constitute any individually
exercisable right with respect to any lands. The persons styled *tolipwaipwaiya* of a tract of land, as descendants of the original pos-
sessors of the land and as predecessors of subsequent generations
of their *dala,* bear as a group a responsibility for the land. The *tolipwaipwaiya* relation is a mythological and genealogical relation to
the soil. To say of a *dala* with respect to a piece of land, "it is their
land," is to recognize the continuity of the *dala* through time such
that all members, living, dead, and yet to be born, are identified as
members of a single group.[6] The *tolipwaipwaiya* relation, like one's
membership in a *dala,* is immutable and nontransferable. Following Malinowski's convention, this relation will be glossed "ownership." But beware: many features of the usual English-language
sense of ownership are embodied in other relations between Trobrianders and their soil.

Nearly every village, as a gardening community, is composed of
more than one hamlet,[7] each hamlet being ideally the residence lo-
cale of the adult males of a *dala* and their nuclear families.[8] A *dala*
often "owns" one or more entire *kwabila.* This situation means
that as a gardening community made up of several hamlets rotates
among its several *kwabila,* during some years a particular *dala* may
"own" a majority of the land under cultivation, yet in other years,
perhaps none. This fact is demonstrated by Malinowski's own data
for Omarakana village[9] and by my observations in Tukwaukwa
village. It is not a requirement of the system that one be an "owner" of land in order to be gardening that land.

USE RIGHTS

The most concrete of the individually exercised legal relations between man and land is a relation usually denoted by the metaphor *iyosi o yamala,* "he holds it in his hand." When a person holds a garden in his hand, whether or not he is an "owner" (member of the "owning" *dala*), he has the right to garden the plot himself or to delegate the gardening of that plot to someone else through a variety of arrangements. This relation will be referred to as "use right."

The metaphor "to hold in his hand" is part of a pervasive set of related metaphors which are used continually in the discussion of land. Gardens as plots of land with fixed boundaries do not move, but to the Trobriander they are in a sense conceptually mobile. When someone does not hold a garden, but does something to get it, it is said that *ikalakova isau,* "he bends over to it, he picks it up." When use rights in a garden are transferred, it may be said of the garden itself that the previous holder *ikilova,* "released it from hand / threw it," *itupi lewa,* "pushed it over there," *ikivisi,* "broke it off [from a cluster of plots]." When use rights in a garden were transferred to a person in a neighboring village, it was said that the garden *lela,* "had gone" to that village. And when use rights to a garden plot held by persons in another neighboring village (thus putting the garden "out of reach") were recovered, it was said of the man who recovered it that *ikosi imeya,* "he picked it [as fruit which is out of reach is picked from trees with a forked pole] and brought it back." Thus, conceptually the garden is located at the person who has use rights to it. As use rights are transferred, the garden is seen as moving relative to people—that is, movement against the backdrop of society rather than geography. Over time, gardens trace paths or *keda* in their movement between persons and groups. These *keda* will turn out to be of critical importance in litigation.

When harvest time nears, people begin to think about which *kwabila* they will be gardening in the following season and what they will have to do to get land to garden there. Each adult male gardener needs land upon which he can make several types of gardens each year. Some of his gardens will provide food for his own household, but the produce of his principal gardens, *kaimata,* will be presented as a harvest gift to another man. By the same token, each gardener will receive at harvest the produce of the *kaimata* of at least one other man. To be told that one has no food or that one must buy food is a serious insult, which reflects not so much on one's gardening abilities as on one's social position. A man who has no one to garden for him is truly despised.

When the stored harvest gifts have been exhausted, the needs of the household are met from the produce of taro gardens, from small yam gardens, and from the cosmetically imperfect yams of the main gardens.

If one has use rights to a *baleku* in the chosen *kwabila,* then one has, of course, the right to garden it oneself or to allow others to garden it. If one has no holdings, one must secure the use of a *baleku.* This is often accomplished by cultivating a yam garden for a person who has rights in the *baleku* to be cultivated. In such an arrangement, the gardener hands over the entire harvest to the holder of the garden.[10] Thus, the gardener satisfies his need to find land on which to cultivate the yams he will present and the rights holder in the garden is assured of someone gardening for him. In such cases, the land holder is likely to be either the headman of the hamlet in which the gardener resides, in which case the exchange garden is due for residence rights in the hamlet, or the father of the gardener, in which case the exchange might be seen as a repayment for the pain of raising the gardener, *velina,* or as an investment in the relation with the father which might later be repaid. Another way to get access to a *baleku* when one has no use rights is through an arrangement called *kaikeda,* a form of sharecropping; in exchange for permission to use the land, the gardener must give a portion of the harvest to the holder of use rights in the land gardened.[11]

When a person exercising use right over a *baleku* chooses not to garden it himself, and delegates the cultivation of the garden to another person instead, that other person—the actual cultivator—does not thereby acquire use rights. He gardens only by the temporary permission of he who "holds the garden in his hand." If one gardens a *baleku* by permission of a person who has use rights in that land, one has considerable autonomy in the actual conduct of the gardening on that plot for the gardening season during which the permission was granted. But unlike the holder of use rights, such a gardener has no legal rights vis-à-vis that *baleku* once the gardening season has ended, and will have to secure such permission again for each subsequent gardening season in which he intends to cultivate that plot. Thus, while the actual gardener of a *baleku* may indeed have enduring and individually exercisable rights to that plot, no enduring legal rights are implied by the simple fact of his gardening it. To be gardening a piece of land is direct evidence of at least, but not necessarily any more than, the fact that one has been granted permission to do so by one who "holds the garden in his hand."

The relation which is here defined as use right is an enduring relation between man and land which can only be initiated or terminated by a formal transfer of the relation from one person to another. It is a relation which is central to a major type of litigation over land.

Since use rights, unlike ownership, are vested in individuals and since individuals move through life cycles, acquiring rights to land as they mature and relinquishing their rights to land as they near death—the final and complete relinquishment—individually exercisable rights to land are by necessity transferable. Having use rights in land, however, does not necessarily imply the right to transfer those rights to another person.

ALLOCATION RIGHTS

The other individually exercised relation between man and land could perhaps be called a meta-right because it is the right to transfer or allocate rights. It is the right to transfer use rights when circumstances arise in which a rights holder relinquishes his claims. This relation is indicated in Trobriand speech by the nominal and verbal forms of the root *karewaga*. As a noun, it can be glossed in English as "authority," "responsibility," "place to decide," "rule," "law," "right," "control." As a verb, it indicates the exercise of such. Henceforth, we will refer to this right as the right of allocation because in the context of land tenure, *karewaga* over land is the right to transfer or allocate rights in land.

The exercise of use rights is tied to the garden work cycle; the use rights to a particular garden will therefore be exercised roughly once in six or seven years. To understand the exercise of the right of allocation, however, we must know more about the process through which rights to land are transferred.

The Transfer of Land Rights

The task of the Trobriand land litigant is to demonstrate the credibility of his own claims to land rights while undermining the credibility of the claims of his opponent. Since claims to individually exercisable rights in land depend upon legitimate transfers of those rights from previous holders, an understanding of how rights to land are transferred is essential to an understanding of land tenure and land litigation.

POKALA

Transfer of rights to land is accomplished through a system called *pokala*. In the most general sense of the word, *pokala* denotes any prestation from an individual of inferior status to one of superior status in the hope, but without the promise, that something will be returned.[12] Traditionally, this general level of usage encompassed several types of events. Major among them are (1) the tribute paid to a chief *guyau* by his subjects,[13] (2) any prestation of wealth, food, or services as an enticement to, or as a rationale for, the reciprocal transfer of either magic, specialized knowledge, a *kula* valuable, or the means of agricultural production (for example, rights to garden lands, betel nut palms, coconut palms, or other fruit trees), and (3) propitiatory offerings to spirits.[14] With the arrival of a colonial government *pokala* took on yet another meaning: the payment of taxes to the government.

The variety of *pokala* which anticipates a reciprocal presentation of rights to gardens or magic is itself distinguished into various types on the basis of the medium of the original prestation. If the medium of *pokala* is the yearly production of an exchange garden in yams, the more specific term *kaivatam* is usually employed. *Kaivatam* is itself a metaphorical usage here, its principal meaning being the poles which are erected next to the sprouting yam and up which the yam vine coils. If the medium of prestation was health care or related services such as mortuary arrangements, then whatever is returned for it is called *yolova*. Such care can be offered in either a terminal or nonterminal illness, but it seems most often evoked as the rationale for a transfer of rights to a garden plot when provided in a terminal illness. If the prestations were a combination of valuables, bananas, fish, and yams, then to designate the medium of exchange only the term *pokala* will do.

There are three types of exchange which involve the medium of valuables, bananas, fish, and yams. In terms of the folk conception of gardens tracing paths through social space, these exchange types are distinguished on the basis of the position and projected movement of the garden plot relative to the "owning" *dala*.

If the rights to the garden plot in question are held by a member of the "owning" *dala,* then any prestations to him in the medium of valuables and so on are designated by the term *pokala*. Such a prestation might legally come either from another member of the "owning" *dala* (for example, a younger brother or a sister's son) or from a member of a different *dala*. If it comes from a member of a different *dala* and the recipient responds by allocating the garden, then the use rights to the garden will pass out of the "owning" *dala* to be held by the provider of the *pokala*. In such a case, the right of allocation remains in the "owning" *dala*. Once the use rights to a garden plot pass out of the hold of the "owning" *dala, pokala* with respect to that plot can be of two types.

If the members of the "owning" *dala* wish the return of the use rights to their land, they may present the nonowner who holds the right of use (who is referred to as a caretaker, *toyamata*) with valuables. Any such prestation is called *katuyumali. Katuyumali* means literally "to cause to return to hand," and when properly executed in the appropriate circumstances that is what it does to the garden vis-à-vis the "owners."

If an heir of the "nonowner" caretaker wishes to acquire the rights of use over the plot following the death of his predecessor who gave *pokala* for it, he must make his prestation in the medium of valuables to the "owners." This is called *katumamata,* which means literally "to cause to wake up" and is conceived of as waking up or refreshing the *pokala* which originally brought the use rights to the land into the hands of the "nonowning" *dala.* Continuing the metaphor, the garden itself in such a case may be referred to as *titavana,* "warmed-up leftover food." This is because keeping use rights in such a garden is not like cooking a whole meal but is like simply warming up one which has already been cooked (prepared) by the *pokala* proper.

Thus, we see in Figure 3 that the term *pokala* as an umbrella term for all of these events contrasts with other terms in a wider domain of exchange.[15] In its more specific readings *pokala* is (1) a member of a contrast set which distinguishes various expected returns, (2) a member of a contrast set, the elements of which distinguish the various media of exchange, and (3) a member of a contrast set, the elements of which distinguish the present and projected social loci of use rights to the garden plot. The context of the utterances in which the term *pokala* occurs is usually but not always sufficient to determine the intended usage.

RESTRICTIONS ON THE ALLOCATION OF THE RIGHT OF ALLOCATION

Each *pokala* type specifies a given set of relations among the participants to the exchange and the garden plot in question. All of the terms described above address the transfer of use rights. But the transfer of use rights is governed by the right of allocation and there are restrictions on the transfer of the right of allocation which do not apply to use rights.

When an "owner" holding use rights and the right of allocation in a *baleku* accepts *pokala* in any medium from a "nonowner" of that *baleku* and use rights are allowed to pass outside the "owning" *dala,* the right of allocation to that *baleku* remains initially with the "owner" who in exercising the right of allocation accepted *pokala* and allowed use rights to the *baleku* to go outside the "owning" *dala.* Ideally, the *karewaga*—right of allocation—over "owned" lands never leaves the owning *dala.* This right can, however, leave the "owning" *dala* in some exceptional circumstances. Being a

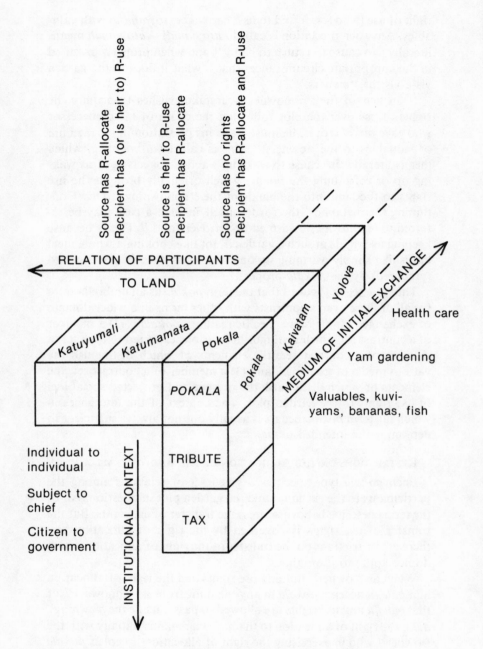

Figure 3. *Marked terms in the domain of* pokala: *three intersecting contrast sets*

matrilineal body, a *dala* depends entirely on its female members for its regeneration.[16] If for any reason no women in the *dala* bear female children, then the *dala* will become extinct, a condition called *wokosi*. When this happens, the last surviving member of the *dala* will take a putative heir (usually from the same major clan) to stand in his stead after his death. Since the "owning" *dala* ceases to exist, the rights in land once held by its members must, of course, now leave that *dala* and be held by members of another *dala*.

Weiner recorded a case in which the right of allocation to a plot of land was permanently alienated from its "owners" when it was given as reparation for a homicide committed by a member of the "owning" *dala* against another *dala*. The expansion of the Tabalu chiefs demonstrates a third way that the right of allocation over land can be alienated from a *dala*. The highest ranking *guyau* (chiefs) in the Trobriands are the Tabalu, who have their headquarters in Omarakana village of Kiriwina district. From this center they have spread their base of power into villages outside of Kiriwina district (Malinowski, 1965, vol. 1, p. 358). Malinowski claimed that the high-ranking Tabalu chiefs were able to expand their holdings in land as they moved into new areas because of the great respect they command among the people of the Trobriands. The prior residents of such an area "surrendered their rights naturally and willingly" to the Tabalu (p. 367). When this happened, Malinowski says, "the titles of the original sub-clan remain dormant and subordinate, but never completely extinct" (p. 368). According to Malinowski, this transfer of rights might be accompanied by some resentment on the part of the previously resident peoples, but their resentment would be tempered with the pride of now being part of a Tabalu village. He observed that Tukwaukwa village was a possible future Tabalu center where this process was in operation in the early part of the century. Malinowski was, of course, looking at this situation from the perspective of the Tabalu of Omarakana with whom he worked most closely. In the interest of completing the description of the mechanism by which rights were acquired by the Tabalu, let me offer the following scenarios constructed by Tukwaukwa villagers reflecting on the period of which Malinowski speaks.

In the old days there were no courts. If a *guyau* saw an exceptional garden belonging to a commoner he would go and grab it. He would just commit his theft and take it away. And we would do nothing to get it back. We fear the axe and the spear.

Suppose you were a commoner and I a *guyau*. You hold land. If I went to you and you did not have any magic, I would take your land. If a

man had powerful magic he could defend himself. Or if he had a powerful group of fierce men he would be able to defend himself and hang
onto his land. If you had none, you would go in fear. I would go to you
who have no strength and take your gardens away. Beautiful though
they may be, I would take them and control them and cut them and eat
them. I would give them to my friends to garden. And you would be left
to find an ugly piece of land wherever you could.

The principle that the right of allocation is always ultimately
exercised by a member of the owning *dala* militates against the
possibility of land being permanently alienated from its *tolipwaipwaiya,* "owners," but as these examples show, that principle can
be violated in a number of circumstances.

The right of allocation over a plot of land is manifested in (1) the
acceptance of *pokala* with respect to that land, (2) making the decision, *kasali,* to actually allocate rights to that land to someone else,
and (3) the responsibility to make *katuyumali* payments to recover
the use rights to that land when they are held by a nonmember of
the "owning" *dala.* The payment of *katuyumali* depends upon
knowledge of the *pokala* conditions under which the use rights to
the garden went out of the owning *dala.* Since that knowledge in
the hands of a legitimate holder of the right of allocation becomes
the power to recover the use rights to the land at a subsequent time
(for example, in an opportunity for *katuyumali*), it is a valuable
resource and is treated as such. In addition to one's actual holdings
in use rights to gardens, one may pass on to succeeding generations
of one's *dala* one's right of allocation over "owned" garden lands
to which others outside the *dala* have acquired use rights. Such
karewaga gives the bearer the right to accept *katumamata* payments—allowing the use rights to the land to remain outside the
"owning" *dala,* and the right and responsibility to recover the use
rights to land by *katuyumali.* Thus, the right of allocation is an
abstract relation between man and land which is transmitted much
as more concrete rights and holdings are, and which under appropriate conditions gives the bearer power over the distribution of the
land resources.

POKALA IN THE DALA

The prototypic *pokala* for land is between maternal kinsmen. An
elderly man of Tukwaukwa village describes it like this: "If our
mother's brother *kadada* is getting old, or perhaps our mother's
mother's brother *tabuda,* we go to him thinking of his magic, his
gardens, his coconut, or betel palms, whatever he has. And on what
evidence will he give them to us? Because we brought him fish, or
valuables, or in gardening if we found many yams and took them to

him. He would see us and think, 'Oh, this man is truly my kinsman,' and those things, his things, he will consent to give us.''

The dynamics of actual bequests are complicated by the fact that
nearly every socially mature man has more than one potential heir.
While Malinowski acknowledged a competition of sorts between
"the son" and "the sister's son," he pays no attention at all to the
fact that there may be many sons, many sister's sons, several
younger brothers, and if the person is old, many sister's daughter's
sons. Moreover, the numbers of persons expected in each of these
categories on the basis of English reckoning of kin must be multi-
plied in the Trobriand system of kinship categorization (Powell,
1956, p. 419). It also must be kept in mind that there is no "rule"
of adelphic succession here. Because of the general correlation between access to resources and one's relative position in the life
cycle, however, older potential heirs are more likely than younger
ones to make successful *pokala*. Malinowski's representation of the
situation was clearly an extreme resorted to in the interest of simple
and clear explanation. Taking the situation to the opposite extreme,
we might imagine virtual armies of potential heirs besieging important men. But this also is not often the case; the establishment of
enduring relations between a man and his heirs depends on the vi-
cissitudes of residence (which, by the way, is primarily viripatrilocal
rather than viriavunculocal)[17] and the personalities and energies of
each. The question becomes, who among those potential heirs
treats the elder in a way that makes him say, "Oh, this man is truly
my kinsman."[18] Thus, a more accurate representation of the actual
situation is that a man who holds magic, valuables, rights to land,
or other resources is likely to have several aspirants to his holdings.
Among those aspirants, none has a "legal" right to anything until
it is allowed by the senior person. Each aspirant must do what he
can to demonstrate his worthiness as an heir and the sincerity of his
relationship to his potential benefactor.

Weiner (1976, p. 157) points out that it is important that an aspirant not declare the nature of his prestations until a substantial debt
is built up and the recipient of the *pokala* asks what the provider
wants in return. At that point, the aspirant tells his elder what he
wants (land, magic, or whatever), and the elder may then decide
whether or not he considers the *pokala* to be sufficient. In such a
case, the elder holds the final say and may refuse to give what is
desired or may instruct the aspirant to deliver more *pokala*.

The prestations which precede the actual declaration of *pokala*
are called *savali*. When several aspirants simultaneously *savali* a
single important man, fierce rivalries sometimes result, and since
one never knows where one stands until the *pokala* is formally de-

clared and either accepted or rejected, there is a possibility of a considerable loss of resources. If, after investing heavily in a *pokala* arrangement, an aspirant is rejected, he has no recourse except, as Powell (1956) says, to "try to persuade his fellows that the older man is unjust and mean" (p. 418) and that they should not *pokala* to him either. It should be obvious from this that *pokala* is not, as Malinowski asserts, an early purchase by the sister's son of what would eventually be his anyway. The prestation of *pokala* is rather a way of providing a holder of resources with a rationale for discriminating among potential recipients in the disbursement of his resources. From another perspective it can be seen as an attempt by a potential heir to induce the holder of rights in land to transfer those rights to him rather than to some other potential heir. I believe this conception of *pokala* explains why it is that when there is but one potential heir (as in a case of *wokosi*), no *pokala* is required. In that case there is no need to distinguish between potential heirs.

The uncertainty of response to *pokala* prestations raises the point that people who deal in land transactions depend heavily on management of information in the field of actors. The strategies of land control are complex, and land controllers give away little information with regard to the disposition of their lands. Good information about past and ongoing land transactions is as important to the aspirant land controller as information about the market is to the stock investor. Land tenure is but one of many spheres of Trobriand life in which knowledge is closely guarded because it manifests itself as power.

POKALA BETWEEN DALA

When *pokala* prestation crosses *dala* boundaries, the transaction is usually accomplished with a single relatively large exchange. Usually, but not always, the headman of the nonowning *dala* makes the *pokala* prestation because he is normally the only one who can marshal sufficient wealth to *pokala* in this medium to another *dala*. Malinowski and Powell maintain that only those members of nonowning *dala* who have residence rights in the village of the "owners" are in a position either legally or logistically to *pokala* for land owned by another *dala*. Where the *kwabila*[19] of adjacent villages share a common boundary, it is possible for use rights in gardens on the boundary to be transferred to members of nonowning *dala* who are not resident in the village of the owners. I recorded two such cases among the villages in the neighborhood of Tukwaukwa village. In each case, when it came time to build a fence around the *kwabila,* the fence was simply rerouted to include the newly acquired garden.

Katuyumali (Return)

The *katuyumali* most often occurs in the context of a mortuary exchange. When the use rights in a piece of land pass out of the "owning" *dala*, they are allowed to do so by the "owners" with the expectation that they will remain out for the remainder of the lifetime of the nonowner who gave *pokala* for the garden, or until in old age he finds no further use for the land. At the death of a person who has given *pokala* and moved use rights to land away from its owners, those of the owners who have rights of allocation to the land present *katuyumali* to the heirs of the nonowner holder and thus retrieve their land.

It is expected that the *katuyumali* will be of roughly equivalent value to the *pokala* which took the garden away from its "owners." However, since no written records are kept, there is no standard unit of currency, and since decades may pass between the *pokala* and the *katuyumali*, it is not possible to verify or reject this expectation. Disputes about the relative magnitudes of the *pokala* and corresponding *katuyumali* frequently arise. Older men often chastise younger men for not appreciating how large the exchanges were in the past.

The information which allows a *dala* to recover its loaned out lands must be maintained inside the *dala*. A knowledgeable, but not wealthy, old man has the following complaint about his potential heirs: "They don't come to me and ask. If I die now, they won't know the lore of these lands. Land snatchers will argue heatedly. They will argue heatedly and take away their lands. They won't pay for it in any way. Their lies alone will get it for them. But [my heirs], would that they might remain *tolipwaipwaiya*, do not ask me that I might speak the *keda* of these lands. They will make mistakes in court and others will take their lands." Since the heirs do not always even know what lands if any are held out of their *dala*, there is usually no direct *pokala* for that information. An elder will give such information to younger members of his *dala* who he feels have treated him well and with respect. They are often those very people who have given him *pokala* hoping for the return of use rights in a garden. An old man who actually holds no use rights to land may still hold the right of allocation to a garden which is held outside the *dala*.

A man may even instruct his son in the disposition of his lands. Upon the man's death, while the son may not be able to take any of the lands himself, and does not have the right of allocation, if he knows the locations and conditions of his late father's lands, he is still an important part of the reallocation process and stands to profit from his involvement.[20]

KATUMAMATA

The *katumamata* (waking up) may also occur in the context of a mortuary distribution, again at the death of the person who has given *pokala* and received use rights in land from its owners. Members of the *dala* of the deceased must pay *katumamata* to the owner having the right of allocation over the land in order to keep using it. The completion of the transaction is at the owner's discretion. The owner may, if he wishes the return of the land and can afford the payment, refuse the *katumamata* and offer *katuyumali* (recovery). The *katumamata* is sometimes, but not always, made by mutual consent of the parties involved. If it occurs before the death of the person who has received use rights in response to *pokala,* a consensus will first be reached between that person and the junior member of his *dala* (the nonowning *dala*) who wishes to succeed him as holder of use rights. If such an agreement is reached, the junior member of the nonowning *dala* may then propose the *katumamata* to the owner who holds the right of allocation over the land in question.

KAIVATAM

The prototypic *kaivatam* relationship is between a son and his father. Gardening for the father is motivated in several ways. First, most young men make their first exchange garden for their fathers.[21] This is because most males reside patrilocally at the time they begin serious gardening on their own, and the father himself is the most likely source of land in the father's hamlet. Second, gardening for one's father is gardening for a spouse of a woman of one's *dala* and is structurally equivalent to what Malinowski and Powell refer to as *urigubu.*[22] It is a way of exercising one's responsibilities as a member of one's *dala* vis-à-vis the husbands of the women in one's *dala*. Finally, it is a way of repaying the father for the care, labor, worry, and resources he has invested in the child in the course of raising it. Such a repayment is called *velina* and is a crucial part of parent-child relationships.

Kaivatam as a relationship evolves over a number of years. Although the receipt of property is often not the motive for entering a *kaivatam* relationship, once such a relationship has been carried on and the recipient decides to bequeath property or resources, the fact of that relationship becomes a perfectly valid rationale for a claim on that property. When a father gives inheritance to a son, it is not, as Malinowski claims, given free. It is given in response to one of several types of exchange relationships likely to exist between father and son. *Kaivatam* does not "purchase" a garden nor is it even a service exchanged for rights to a garden. It is rather a socially responsible act which can be interpreted by a parent who is so inclined as a valid rationale for reciprocation. The notion of a "free gift" is quite alien to the Trobriand ethos.

YOLOVA

The prototypic *yolova* is between brothers-in-law, with a man caring for his sister's husband *lubola* in the illness of the latter; *yolova* is also common between parents and their children, especially in the old age of the parents. Any debilitating illness or injury which renders the victim incapable of caring for himself and thus in need of care by others presents an opportunity for the initiation of such a relationship. When the period of care ends, either in the death or recovery of the victim, those who have provided health-related services will be paid in a distribution ceremony, *sagali*. Strictly speaking, it is the payment for service, not the service rendered, which is called *yolova*. When the *dala* of the person cared for does not have sufficient resources available to make immediate payment for the services rendered, the use rights to a garden may be given as a temporary payment to be replaced later by a payment in another exchange medium. Use rights in a garden received as *yolova* are not held for life, as are rights received in response to other types of *pokala*. Use rights which leave the "owning" *dala* in temporary payment as *yolova* can be recovered by the "owning" *dala* as soon as they acquire sufficient wealth to make the payment in valuables. A complication was noted by Powell (1956): "Such care ... may be recognized by the receiver as *pokala* in his lifetime, or may be claimed to have been such in effect by those who gave it after his death and against his estate" (p. 420).

Up to this point, we have considered land control by males only. While the vast majority of land transactions are among men, there exist circumstances by which women come to hold rights in land. Except for *yolova,* however, women usually lack access to the resources which would allow them to acquire land by formal *pokala*. Women acquire land primarily by bequest as a gift of affection from father, mother's brother, or brother. In such a case, the women's attentions to the men's needs are as *pokala*. Whatever she does to become the "true personal kinsperson" of a man qualifies as *pokala*. A garden held by a woman is referred to by the marked construction *bilekuvivila*—literally, "garden of a woman."

CONSUMMATION OF RIGHTS TRANSFER: KASALI

In every type of *pokala* relation except *katuyumali* (recovery), which under proper conditions cannot be refused, the recipient in the person of an owner with rights of allocation makes the decision regarding the transfer of rights in land. The exercise of the right of allocation through the assignment of rights in land to a person who has presented any form of *pokala* is denoted by the verb *kasali.* Such an assignment of rights to land needs to be made public to some extent for it to stand relative to other possible claims. In cases of *pokala* in the medium of valuables, the decision is often accompanied by a clinching payment witnessed by the blood kin of the provider and the recipient of *pokala.* In cases where the transfer is part of a mortuary ceremony, there are, of course, witnesses present. For decisions in response to *kaivatam,* the *kasali* itself is often not made in public. This is not out of any intention to secrecy but simply because gardens which are transferred under such circumstances tend to be gardens for which no one else has presented a more formal type of *pokala.*

Garden plots which have not yet been allocated to someone else by a holder of rights in them are called *tupwa* (extra, spare, of leftover) with respect to their holder. When rights to a garden are transferred to another person, that is, when the holder of rights of allocation in a garden *kasali*'s it, the garden's status changes from *tupwa* (extra) to *kasesila* (allocated) with respect to that holder. As long as a garden is *tupwa,* it is accessible to all types of *pokala.*

Upon the death of an owner who has rights in land, those of his gardens which are still *tupwa* (following the settlement of claims against his estate) revert to the person referred to by Malinowski and Powell as the "headman" of the *dala.* That the headman takes *tupwa* gardens and rights to gardens by default is an important principle which again points out that *pokala* is not the early purchase by the sister's son of what would eventually be his anyway. Unless that sister's son happens also to be the headman of the land holder's hamlet, he receives no lands without making *pokala* for them. Even if he is the headman, he may want to *pokala* to his predecessor for a particularly desirable piece of land to ensure that it is not *kasali*'ed to someone else first. Desirable land is especially unlikely to be left as *tupwa* upon the death of the rights holder.

Default control of *tupwa* lands is one of the headman's primary advantages over other important men in the *dala.* Because of the many obligations of the office, however, headmanship may in some cases be a net disadvantage.

THE INTERPERSONAL POLITICS OF POKALA

Pokala relations between the holders of resources and persons who aspire to those resources are not legal contractual arrangements. To see them only as legal obligations is to miss both the emotional texture of the relationships, which is itself a major determinant of the volume of tokens exchanged, and the freedom of choice available to rights holders and aspirants in the formation and maintenance of such relations. Every exchange event is a communication from one person to another of both an artifact (item exchanged) and a social message. The movement of artifacts makes exchange important economically. The participant's interpretations of social messages makes exchange important symbolically.

Not every son makes an exchange garden for his father—many sons attach themselves to others with resources—but a son who does diligently make a yearly exchange garden for his father is making a social statement which must please his father, and in the eyes of a Trobriander, makes the father want to reciprocate. Likewise, the sister's son who takes fish, valuables, and yams to his mother's brother, while imposing no legal obligation on his mother's brother, is believed, in the words of my informants, to "sweeten his mind" and dispose him to reciprocation.

It is not legally required that any man make *pokala* prestations to his mother's brother. It is a volitional decision on the part of the *pokala* provider. At the outset, the social message of such prestations is one of deference, respect, and desired association. Malinowski's characterization of the emotional contrast between father-son relations and mother's brother-sister's son relations is surely exaggerated. Bonds of real affection do exist in many mother's brother-sister's son relationships; an elder man, however, does not part lightly with hard-won resources and likes to see an indication of enduring loyalty before he considers awarding them to someone else. This is in part why it is considered in bad taste for a potential heir to declare his intent for *pokala*. To do so is to change the social message of the exchange (from deference to venality) and to force the contractual aspect of the relation. The introduction of that contractual aspect properly belongs with the recipient of the *pokala,* not with its provider. Also, the real measure of *pokala* of any kind is not its physical magnitude but the extent to which it convinces the recipient that the provider is his "true kinsman."

With young men in competition for attachment to important older men and older men having varying opinions of their juniors, it sometimes happens that such exchange relations are terminated. A young man may "turn his back" on an elder if he feels he can establish a more profitable alliance elsewhere. Such dissolutions often cause some enmity in either or both parties.

The man who has operative exchange relations with one or more of his own sons and one or more of his sister's sons may give parts of his holdings to both groups within the legal constraints imposed by the principles of transfers of rights discussed above. Such an apportionment is, however, probably not fruitfully represented as a conflict between "the patriarchal and matriarchal principle" (Malinowski, 1965, vol. 1, p. 360). From the point of view of the Trobriander, at least, for such an elder *not* to make this apportionment would be seen as a failure to meet social responsibility. This is clear when we realize that the transfer of rights in land to any particular individual is not a foregone social conclusion but rather a response to one or more of the several types of *pokala* which are intended to induce such a transfer.

Titles in Land

A "title" in land may be defined as the combination of one or more simultaneously held relations between a person and a particular unit of territory. Without regard to the principles of transfer of rights in land, there would be eight possible titles in land. Figure 4 shows these eight titles as terminal nodes in a binary branching tree.

The principle that the right of allocation is to be exercised only by members of the owning *dala* prunes nodes five and six out of the tree. These are titles which in principle cannot exist, because there is normally no way any person could come to simultaneously hold the relations to land they represent. A person cannot be a non-owner of a unit of land and yet have the right of allocation over it. All of the other titles are possible in accordance with the principles of transfers of rights in land.

Node 1 represents the combination of rights and relations to land which correspond best to our English language notion of ownership. The reasons for my reluctance in following Malinowski in referring to simple *tolipwaipwaiya* (node 4) as "owners" can be easily seen in this figure. The title represented by node 1 is actually a combination of the *tolipwaipwaiya* relation with both of the individually exercisable rights to land. It is thus much closer to our sense of ownership than the *tolipwaipwaiya* relation by itself. This title is expressed in common discourse by the compounds *tolibaleko* or *tolikwabila* (depending on the size of the unit of land), *tolivavagi* (*vavagi* for the abstract "thing"), or by the phrase *la vavagi titolela* ("his thing by himself"). The compounds which specify a unit of land (*baleko, kwabila*) as opposed to the generic "land" (*pwaipwaiya*) denote individually exercisable relations. To say *tolipwaipwaiya* implies the same diffuse relation of all members of a given *dala* to all of that *dala*'s lands. The specification of a cultivable and economically appropriated unit of land with *toli-* prefix implies an individually exercisable right with respect to that land.

Given that Malinowski (1965) read *tolipwaipwaiya* and *tolibaleko* as indicative of the same vague level of relationship, it is not

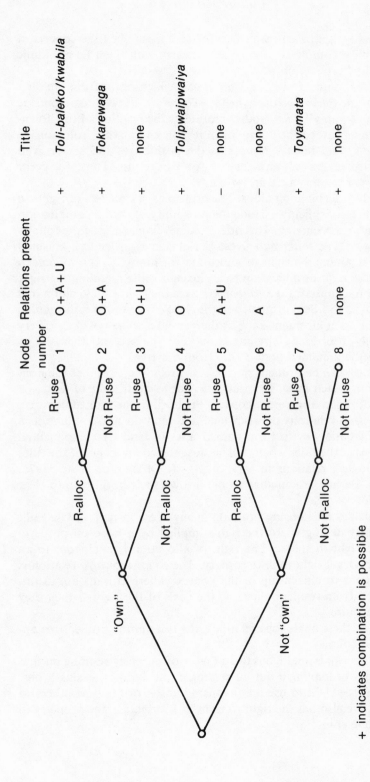

Figure 4. *Complete title tree*

surprising that he erroneously concluded that "the titles concerned are almost completely honorific and carry with them no economic benefits" (vol. 1, p. 345).

Nodes 2 and 7 in Figure 3 are a pair which result from the division of the *tolibaleko* title when use rights are allowed to go outside of the "owning" *dala*. Node 2 represents the position of the "owner" who awarded the use rights in response to *pokala* from outside the *dala,* and node 7 represents the position of the person who provided the *pokala* and got use rights in return. Thus, for every *toyamata* there is a *tokarewaga.*

Node 3 is a bit anomalous. The principles of transfers of rights in land do not explicitly exclude the possibility of such a combination of relations occurring. This title could develop in any of the following ways: (1) a *tolibaleko* gives use rights in a garden to a kinsman while retaining the right of allocation for himself; (2) a *tolibaleko* gives the right of allocation to a kinsman while retaining the right of use for himself; (3) a *tolibaleko* gives the right of allocation to a garden to another kinsman, and the right of use in the same garden to a different kinsman. Each of these events, while possible, is very unlikely in ordinary circumstances. For the present, then, let us prune the unnamed node 3 title from our tree.

Node 8 can be pruned, since it is the relation, or rather the non-relation, which most Trobrianders bear to most units of land.

The pruned title tree is shown in Figure 5. In the pruned title tree, recognized relations between men and land do not combine in a paradigmatic way to form named titles in land. A componential analysis of the titles would fail because the components of the titles have logical relations to each other (cf. D'Andrade et al., 1972, p. 51). Perhaps an analogy from our own society will help to clear this up.

Consider the housing situation in any Western nation. Use right is closely analogous to the rights implied by a lease on property with a right to sublet. The right of allocation is analogous to an owner's legal right to sell property. The *tolipwaipwaiya* relation is analogous to citizenship in the context where citizens are distinguished from resident aliens on the basis of the rights which they may acquire.

Given these analogous relations, the titles in the pruned tree appear as follows:

Tolibaleko is analogous to an owner of property residing on that property or loaning it out, or renting it out, but not leasing it out. He has the right to use the premises himself or to allow others to use it. He also has the right to transfer his rights in the property to someone else.

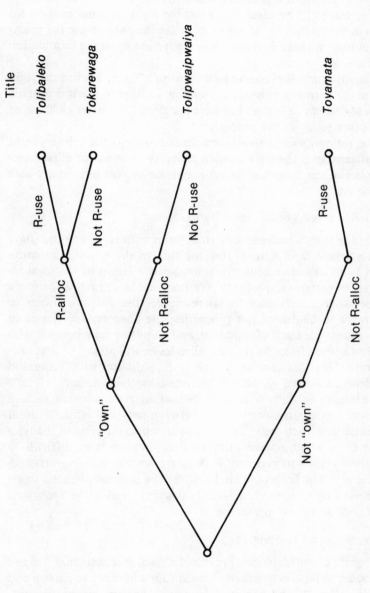

Figure 5. *Pruned title tree*

The *tokarewaga* is analogous to an absentee landlord or lessor. He has allowed someone else to lease the property or has purchased the property from a previous landlord who has allowed someone else to lease it. The *tokarewaga* has the right to transfer (sell) his right in the property but he does not have the right to use the premises himself without first recovering that right upon the termination of the lease.

The *toyamata* is of course analogous to a lessee. He has the right to use the premises himself, or to allow another to use it through a sublet (*kaikeda*). He does not have the right to transfer (sell) his or any other rights in the property.

The *tolipwaipwaiya* is a citizen. In this analogy the primary right of citizenship is the right to own property. A resident alien (non-member of the "owning" *dala*) may lease or rent but cannot own property.

THE ELUSIVE TROBRIAND "OWNER"

This analogy illustrates one final point with regard to the study of Trobriand land tenure. Imagine that in the housing situation there is no hall of records containing specifications of the legal relations of persons to property. We find that in normal discourse a homeowner in reference to his residence, the absentee owner in reference to his leased out properties, the alien resident lessee in reference to his place of residence, and even the young boarder who sublets a room from the resident alien lessee will all say of that residence, "This is my house." Such is the situation with Trobriand gardeners and their gardens. When one asks, "Whose land is this?" there might truthfully be as many as four different answers, each in reference to a particular relation between men and land. Without recourse to written records or without an understanding of the relations from which named titles are composed, it is as difficult to interpret claims to property in Western society housing arrangements as it is in Trobriand land tenure. The nonparadigmatic intersection of rights to land in named titles truly makes the Trobriand "owner" an elusive personage.

FREQUENCIES OF EVENTS

From the considerations presented above, it is clear that it is not necessary to have even use rights to any land in order to garden and survive. Powell and Malinowski assert that important persons, *guyau*s and headmen often hold a majority of the lands gardened by a village. Powell (1956, appendix table 15) reports that sixty-two percent of those who are neither *guyau*s nor *dala* headmen in Omarakana village claim rights in garden plots. That leaves thirty-eight percent with no rights in land. Since Powell only reports "holdings," meaning use rights, we cannot know for sure how many of those gardens are held by *tolibaleku* and how many by *toyamata*. Omarakana is of course the village of the most powerful *guyau* in the Trobriand group. My observations agree with Malinowski's assessment that "in communities of low rank, there is, on the whole, a much greater variety of ownership" (vol. 1, p. 372). Even so, holding land is a level of power, wealth, and prestige which is simply not achieved by all persons even in villages of low rank.

The *pokala* arrangements described above as roads to the acquisition of land are not traveled with equal frequency. The standard *pokala* inside the "owning" *dala* is by far the most frequent rationale for the transfer of rights in land. Powell (1956, appendix table 16) reports that about eighty percent of the transfers are within the *dala* while twenty percent are transfers between *dala*. These data fit the informants' notions that the prototypic *pokala* is between a man and his mother's brother or his mother's mother's brother.

Regardless of the rationale for transfer of land, the vast majority of garden plot transfers are accomplished smoothly and never come into open dispute. Of the nearly one hundred garden plots gardened by the men of Tukwaukwa village in 1976, only three were brought into court for resolution of their status through litigation.

The Institutional Context of Litigation

The village court system which provides the institutional context for the litigation discussed here is a syncretic convention combining the traditional village airing of disputes with a hearing protocol and authority structure introduced first by the British and later by the Australian colonial governments. In the early days of the colonial administration both criminal and civil cases were brought before the resident magistrate. In civil cases such as land disputes, however, this sometimes caused more trouble than it cured. The resident magistrate at the time of Malinowski's arrival in the Trobriands refused to hear land disputes, knowing that he lacked the knowledge required to render satisfactory judgment. "His successor, who had no experience in administrative work, adopted a method natural to the European but fatal in a matrilineal community. He would enquire whose father had cut the disputed garden in olden days, a question which, under matrilineal descent, was beside the point and usually admitted of no answer, since the fathers of both litigants probably belonged to other communities" (Malinowski, 1965, vol. 1, p. 103).

Modern-day Trobrianders say that the recognition that the government officers were incapable of producing decisions which were satisfactory to the parties involved led to the present system of hearing civil cases in the village court presided over by the *guyau* of the local district. The *guyau* is appropriate as the head of the court because by virtue of political position a *guyau* has the authority to back up his decisions with effective sanctions and because part of a *guyau*'s training for the job is in learning the *liliu,* sacred myths, which are needed to assess claims of groups to particular parcels of land.

Criminal cases are still handled by the administration. At present the administration presence is limited to a few local police and the office of the assistant provincial commissioner.

While the present institutional context of litigation contains elements of European court procedure, the practice of quarreling over land at the time of cutting the gardens predates contact. Malinowski reports that during his stay in the Trobriands, "there were long *yakala,* native litigations, arising out of disputes at cutting" (p. 103). Unfortunately, Malinowski seems not to have witnessed any of these *yakala* first-hand and gives no description of their workings at all.

In the absence of an institutionalized forum for litigation, transactions in land between *dala* must have been very dangerous indeed. Then more than now, success in litigation must have depended upon verbal intimidation and force of character. When *yakala* failed, disputes over land are said to have been settled by sorcery and the spear. In fact, when questioned about the nature of litigation prior to the establishment of the village courts, villagers express most concern not about agreed upon transactions among peers but about the inability to defend against the encroachment of powerful chiefs. Given the commoners' perspective on the nature of transactions in land, it is no wonder that they praise the introduction of the village court system.

Types of Litigation

Nowadays Trobrianders distinguish two major types of dispute over land: those in which an individual's right to garden a particular plot is at issue and those in which a *dala*'s claim as owners of the land is at issue. The latter are by far the more serious of the two types. This should be clear from the fact that in a dispute within a *dala*, the outcome will affect the futures of the individuals involved but the overall situation of the *dala* vis-à-vis its land is not threatened. In a dispute between *dala*, however, the future productive power of an entire *dala* is threatened.

When a case involves a dispute between *dala,* the question to be decided will be, "With which group is this land truly associated?"

Weiner (1976, pp. 40-43) describes such a case. The decision will be made on the basis of the litigants' abilities in reciting the genealogy of the land from the time of their ancestors' first involvement with it to the present. Such accounts may include recitations of the origin myths of the groups and the "details of the social relations established during the course of finding land" (p. 41).

When a case involves claims by individuals to use rights in a garden, the decision will be made on the basis of the litigant's ability to produce a credible history of transactions in land which culminates in his having gained rights in the land. Such a history will typically trace the *keda* (path of social movement) of the garden only a few generations back to some previous rights holder whose claim is acknowledged by both litigants.

According to Malinowski the theme of quarreling over gardens is frequent in folklore. He reports a portion of the myth of Kudayuri in which a dispute over the use of a parcel of land results in a man murdering his older brother (vol. 1, p. 104). I do not know whether such crimes are actually ever committed, but it is clear from post-case discussions with defeated litigants that such notions are very much on their minds. In the case of a dispute between *dala,* the outcome might be much more serious than the death of an individual. Malinowski's maps of the Trobriands show a village called Dubwaga located about midway down the coral ridge that runs the length of the eastern edge of the island. All that remains of that village today are the heavy coral boulders which once supported the corners of the *liku* (ceremonial yam houses). The two *dala* which used to inhabit the place are said to have decimated each other through sorcery because of chronic disputes about the control of the village lands. After many years of retributory killings, the few survivors finally dispersed and moved into other villages.

3 | The Model

WHAT SORTS OF INFERENCES can we make about reasoning from an examination of natural discourse? One might think that it is possible to apply the rules of symbolic logic directly to discourse to determine whether or not the discourse conforms to the standards of logical thought. As Quine (1960) points out, however, the fact that an English speaker utters the phrase "Yes and no" in response to a question in context is not prima facie evidence that the speaker is being illogical in spite of the fact that the utterance contains what is apparently the baldest of contradictions. Intelligent interpretation, which Quine considers a form of translation, assumes that the two parts of the statement have different referents and are therefore not in contradiction. The same sort of problem is of course present in the interpretation or translation of any piece of natural discourse. The sort of literal translation that takes the phrase above to be illogical has also been applied at times to utterances taken from other cultures and used as evidence that the natives are irrational. The literal translation of figurative language can lead to the same sort of error. This was the case, for example, with Beattie's (1966) interpretation that the Nuer (Sudanese) statement "Twins are birds" is self-contradictory. As Quine says, "Wanton translation can make natives sound as queer as one pleases. Better translation imposes our logic upon them and would beg the question of prelogicality if there were a question to beg" (p. 58).

This notion that better translation imposes our logic upon the natives is important because if that is the case, then we will never fail to find the natives logical. We can pursue this question quite naturally with respect to the Trobriands by following Quine's own footnote: "Malinowski, pp. 68 ff., spared his islanders the imputation of prelogicality by so varying his translations of terms, from occurrence to occurrence, as to sidestep contradiction" (p. 58).

Quine gives no examples of offending variations in translations, but his remarks raise some vital issues. What makes a translation better? What might be the source of the variation in Malinowski's translations? Quine suggests that it is adherence to a rule that contradiction is not to be allowed. It seems to me that there is another reason: Malinowski recognized or understood (he need not have been able to articulate his understanding) the nature of the logical relations that obtain between the propositions involved. These relations are a permanent part of the belief structure which underlies communication. In spoken communication in particular, the meaning of a message is not in the message itself. The meaning is in the interpretation of the message. The interpretation is accomplished by reference to a large body of conceptual material that seldom finds explicit representation in the spoken messages of the speech community. The reliance on implicit conceptual material is perhaps less important in the interpretation of written texts than it is in the case of spoken language.

In translation of natural discourse the translator must first parse the utterance into its representation in the conceptual structure of the source culture (that is, the culture surrounding the language to be translated). It may be that there is nothing in the conceptual structure of the target culture (that is, the culture surrounding the language into which the utterance is being translated) that corresponds to the relevant items in the source culture. Where that is the case, those conceptual entities will have to be built up before the translation can be properly understood. The listener will be ready to understand a translation only when he has a conceptual structure that corresponds with that of the source culture. When the listener has such a structure, he can use the lexical semantics of the target language to map the translation onto an appropriate conceptual structure. This is why Malinowski argued that translation can only be meaningfully rendered in the context of ethnography and, I think, why his translations of terms vary from occurrence to occurrence, context to context. Given that the logical connectives of one language may not cover precisely the same ground as that covered by those of another language (Trobriand, for instance, has no equivalent for the simple conjunction "and"), it may be necessary in the course of generating a translation that will be meaningful to its intended audience to vary the translations of particular logical connectives. This does not, however, mean that we will necessarily impose our logic on them.

In the course of making a meaningful translation, the translator will of course have to employ the lexicon of logical connectives that is available in the target language. The question of logic in this perspective is not about language but about the conceptualizations that are evoked by language. As analysts we have an opportunity to impose our logic on the natives not so much in the translation of language per se as in whatever we do to cause our readers to generate a conceptual structure that they can use to make sense of the translation. If the ethnographer errs in the presentation of the principles that underlie the discourse, the reported discourse may still map nicely onto those principles, but its meaning—the understanding it evokes in the reader—will be different from the understanding evoked in the native by the original.

Quine (1960) has argued for a set of semantic criteria for the translation of logical connectives. For example, "The semantic criterion of negation is that it turns any short sentence to which one will assent into one from which one will dissent" (p. 57). In theory, such a procedure ought to be sufficient to decide the meaning of a connective. In practice, however, things are seldom that simple. The interpretation of the meanings of logical connectives in natural discourse involves issues of pragmatics as well as semantics. The following example from Fillenbaum (1977) illustrates this point: "Thus, 'If you do that I'll shoot you' may be paraphrased as 'Do that and I'll shoot you' or as 'Don't do that or I'll shoot you' " (p. 64).

Here a single underlying relation between two simple propositions is expressed via three different logical connectives. The speaker's choice of a connective depends upon pragmatic considerations such as which proposition he wishes to make salient, which truth values he wishes each proposition to appear with, and so on. "What is important is not only that a message be true, but that it have a point in context, and understanding the point of a message will often require that one go beyond what is said literally and beyond truth-functional considerations" (Fillenbaum, 1977, p. 84).

I do not believe there is any simple direct translation of logical connectives. This is the case because logic is an appropriate metalanguage for the organization of the structures to which natural language points, but not for natural language itself. In fact, it seems that deciding on a set of direct translations of logical connectives is one way to produce a "wanton" translation that can make the natives seem queer.

With respect to this issue we again find that the Trobrianders have figured in the literature of primitive thought. It is hard to imagine a more wanton translation than that given to the Trobriand logical connectives by Lee (1940, 1949). Working exclusively from Malinowski's published materials, Lee decided on a set of direct translations for Trobriand logical connectives that was based on an examination of the connectives' homonyms. Giving each connective the literal meaning of a homonym (for example, *uula* means "base" as well as "cause"), Lee claimed that the language of the Trobriands lacked terms which denote logical relations among propositions. From this she concluded that "this does not mean that the Trobrianders are incapable of explaining a sequence in terms of cause and effect, but rather that this relationship is of no significance" (1949, p. 407). Lee's denial of the concept of causality led her to assert that Trobrianders not only do not interpret acts in terms of the intents of actors, but they do not even have intents. "The Trobriander performs an act because of the act itself, not for its effects" (p. 408). She concluded her paper as follows: "Whether they are given or read into reality by us, temporality, causation, teleology, and relationship in general have neither meaning nor relevance for Trobriand behavior" (p. 415).

Lee arrived at these conclusions without knowledge of the Trobriand language and without having set foot on Trobriand soil. A more reasonable set of meanings for the most common Trobriand logical connectives is given below.

(1) *kidamwa*
    (a) "if" as it appears in "if, then" conditionals.
    (b) "as if": *Isakaigu, kidamwa lubegu,* "He gave it to me, as if he is my friend."
    (c) "in order to": *Ila o laodina kidamwa bitaii kaivatam,* "He went into the forest in order to cut yam poles."

(2) *mwada*
    (a) "if only" desired hypothetical presupposes a disjunction from the present focus state: *Mwada kaitala dawaga,* "If only we had a canoe." Presupposes that we do not have a canoe.

(3) *kaina*
    (a) disjunction, "or": *Bala, kaina bukula?* "Shall I go or shall you?"
    (b) "perhaps": *Kaina bimeya buwa,* "Perhaps he will bring betelnut."
    (c) with questioning intonation indicates doubt: *Yokwa bukula, kaina?* "Aren't you going?"

(4) *mitaga*
    (a) exclusive disjunction, "or": *Desi! Mitaga bawem,* "Stop or I'll hit you."

   (b) result counter to expectations, "but": *Lanigada, mitaga
       ikatulakaigu,* "I begged, but he refused me."
   (c) strong endorsement, when given a challenging questioning
       intonation in response to a question means "What else?"
       or "But of course!"
   (d) pointer to unmet expectations: *Mitaga yegu?!* "What about
       me?!"

(5) *pela*
   (a) "reason," "goal," "end": *Ima pela magila bikaiyaku,*
       "He came because he wanted to talk."
   (b) *avaka pela,* "What reason? Why?"

(6) *uula*
   (a) "basis," "source," "cause": *uulela mokwita,* "the true
       cause."
   (b) *avaka uula?* "What cause? Why?"
   Both *pela* and *uula* also occur in demonstrative forms, *mapela*
   and *mauula,* which can be glossed "therefore."

(7) There is no logical particle corresponding to the English con-
    junction "and." Conjunction is accomplished by:
   (a) apposition of arguments: *Mekuvi, Kwemwai itataiisi,* "Me-
       kuvi and Kwemwai cut it."
   (b) use of the lexemes *deli,* "together with," or *tuvela,* "more/
       in addition."
   (c) for sentient arguments by use of the proximally possessed
       noun *so,* "companion": *Matona sola la kwava,* literally,
       "that man companion (his) his wife," or freely, "He and
       his wife."

   This list of the uses to which the most frequent Trobriand logical
connectives are put again illustrates the extent to which pragmatic
considerations enter the interpretation of the meaning of a connective in discourse.
   The point of all of this is two-fold. First, if we are to understand
natural discourse we will need to know what the logical relations
are that these connectives of discourse point to. Second, if we are to
understand how discourse is understood, we will have to have a
way to explicitly represent these logical relations.

Notation

   The most important thing to expect of a notation is that it accu-
rately encode the information desired and that it behave in a way

that is isomorphic with the system it supposedly describes. In some basic sense, all of the available models of semantic information processing are probably equally far from describing what is actually going on in people's minds. There are, however, differences among them in the degree to which their simulations of human performance seem natural. They also differ in the ease of use and understanding. Many of the models which have been implemented as computer programs have running versions that are written in a computer language (usually a list-processing language) and publication versions which are simply notations that express in a way that is intelligible to the reader what the program is about. I have not attempted to make this study a project in artificial intelligence. I have developed a notation in which the propositions of discourse about land can be explicitly represented and with which the use of the logical relations among propositions can be demonstrated, but I have not taken the next step of developing a computer program.

In a propositional representation, semantic information is encoded as a network of *concepts* interconnected by *relations*. Concepts are specific instances in the domain of discourse. In this domain of discourse, for example, a particular person, say John, or a particular garden plot, say the garden plot named Riverbank, are represented as simple concepts. The relation "holds use rights in" can link these concepts together to form the proposition "John holds use rights in Riverbank." The relation "holds use rights in" obviously obtains between many people and many units of land. In fact, this relation always links one instance from the range of concepts that are people to one instance from the range of concepts that are economically appropriatable units of land. When a relation is stated in terms of such variable ranges as these, it is a *schema*. When the ranges are replaced by concepts (a process called *instantiation* because it is the assignment of specific instances to the relation) the schema becomes a *proposition*. A schema is then a form or a template from which an arbitrarily large number of propositions can be constructed.

Propositions have two very important properties. First, since they stand for specific entities and events in the domain of discourse, they are themselves concepts and may be linked by relations to other concepts. This allows propositions to nest within each other. Second, propositions differ from both schemata and simple concepts in that a proposition may have a truth value associated with it. Basic concepts like "John" either correspond to something in the world or they do not, but they are neither true, false, likely, or unlikely. Schemata also are neither true nor false.

Consider the familiar relation in mathematics called "greater than." This relation obtains between two variables. Following the conventions of mathematics, we write the relation as "x greater than y," where x and y each denote the range of real numbers. Obviously the relation is neither true nor false as it stands. When particular instances of x and y are chosen from the appropriate range, however, the relation can be interpreted as making an assertion about the domain of discourse. That assertion, a proposition, can be assigned a truth value—in this case, either true or false depending upon the values of x and y.

The propositions that constitute the relevant domain of discourse in this study involve rights in land and the events which control transfers of rights, namely, *pokala* and *kasali*. The relations from which these propositions can be generated are given below with their variable ranges.

Right(s) in land [person, unit of land]

pokala [person$_1$, person$_2$, things exchanged]

Allocate [person$_1$, person$_2$, Right(s) in land]

The following notation has been developed to express the schemata and propositions:

Variables and concepts: A set of square brackets, [   ], will represent the range of persons. When the set of brackets is labeled, it will represent a particular instance of the range, that is, the concept which is a particular person. The lower-case letter g will represent the range of garden plots. Particular gardens will be represented by their proper names or abbreviations of proper names.

Relations: Individually exercisable rights in a garden will be represented by a function notation. $A(g)$ = right of allocation over a garden. $U(g)$ = use rights in a garden. $A + U(g)$ = right of allocation and use rights in a garden.[1] The notation $R(g)$ will be applied where there is uncertainty about which rights are involved. The relation "A person holds use rights in a garden" will be written in this notation as [U(g)]. This is, by the way, a direct encoding of the *toyamata* title. The other important titles are *tokarewaga*, [A(g)], and *tolibaleku*, [A + U(g)]. The "ownership" relation will be represented by an area in the diagram which is labeled "owners" and separated from the nonowners by a dotted line. Thus, the proposition "John holds the right of allocation over the garden Riverbank, and Bill has use rights in Riverbank" would appear in this notation as follows:

"owners"	:	"nonowners"
John	:	Bill
[A(RivBk)]	:	[U(RivBk)]

Pokala events will be represented by a labeled arrow drawn from the brackets denoting the provider to those denoting the recipient.

$$
\begin{array}{c}
pokala \\
[R(g)] \longleftarrow \quad [\quad]
\end{array}
$$

When the content of the *pokala* is specified, it will be indicated under the arrow.

$$
\begin{array}{c}
pokala \\
[R(g)] \longleftarrow \quad [\quad] \\
kaivatam
\end{array}
$$

Allocation events will be represented by an arrow drawn from the allocator to the recipient. The arrow will be labeled with the rights transferred. Thus, the relation "Someone allocates use rights in a garden to someone else" will be written,

$$
\begin{array}{c}
U(g) \\
[\quad] \longrightarrow [\quad]
\end{array}
$$

The inclusion of the notation for the exchange events allows the expression of a number of more complicated propositions. For example, the complex proposition "John gave *pokala* in the form of a yearly yam garden (*kaivatam*) to Mary, who holds the right of allocation and use rights in the garden called Chrysalis" can be written in this notation as

$$
\begin{array}{ccc}
\text{Mary} & pokala & \text{John} \\
[A + U(Chry)] & \longleftarrow & [\qquad\qquad] \\
& kaivatam &
\end{array}
$$

Propositions which are asserted to be false will be preceded or followed by a capital letter F. Thus if someone asserted that the proposition above was false, that assertion would appear in the notation as

$$
\begin{array}{cccc}
& \text{Mary} & pokala & \text{John} \\
F & [A + U(Chry)] & \longleftarrow & [\qquad\qquad] \\
& & kaivatam &
\end{array}
$$

This notation was chosen over a more traditional list structure or propositional "polish notation" because it economically encodes otherwise unwieldy propositions and because the spatial component of the representation naturally echoes the prominent metaphor of the movement of gardens across a social landscape.

In such systems, in addition to propositions being embedded

within each other, propositions can be conjoined to form larger propositions. The component pieces can be assembled into a general schema for the transfer of rights in land. Assuming a consistent assignment of concepts throughout (for example, all the sets of brackets in the left column denote the same unspecified instance from the range of persons), the general schema is as follows:

[R(g)]
　　　　　　　　pokala
　[R(g)]　◄────　[　]

　　　　　　　R(g)
　[　]　────►　[　]
　　　　　　　[R(g)]

This structure differs from the schemata which represent other types of *pokala* (to chief, to government, to *baloma*) only in the specification of the expected return. Further, it can be seen as a subtype of a more general schema for relations of social reciprocity in general. These structural similarities suggest that a large number of such schemata can be built from a general template such as that for reciprocity. The advantage of this is that in acquisition and storage, the information processing load is much reduced if the structures themselves can be derived from a master rather than having to be learned and stored as complete structures in isolation from each other. This is an important consideration in a system that has limited memory resources.

Of course this representation only encodes the skeleton of what the concepts of reciprocity or *pokala* actually involve. It gives only a very mechanical rendering of the understanding that goes into interpretations of acts in this domain, but the mechanism encoded is one that can successfully model the inferences that people make about propositions representing entities in the world of land litigation.

The general or master schema can be instantiated in every detail by assigning concepts from the appropriate ranges to the variables. The result would be a single complex proposition representing a complete transfer of rights. Such a proposition will be called an *episode*. Episodes are the basic units of discourse in this domain.

In the ethnographic description of transfers of rights in land these simple propositions were linked to each other by more abstract relations that resist ostensive definition. These are the functional relations that specify what leads to what and what causes what. Consider the case of two members A and B of a single *dala*:

If the propositions
"A has rights of allocation and use   A
in a garden"   [A + U(g)]
and   *pokala*   B
"B gives *pokala* to A"   [A + U(g)] ◄——— [   ]
are true,
then it might also be true that
"A allocates his rights in the   A + U(g)
garden to B"   [   ] ———► [   ]
and if that is true,
it will cause the proposition
"B has rights of allocation and
use in the garden"   [A + U(g)]
to be true.

Person A may, however, decide not to allocate rights to B in spite of B's *pokala*. The first two propositions being jointly true, therefore, permit but do not cause the third proposition to be true. If either of the first two propositions is false, that is,

If either
"A hasn't any rights in the garden"   F   [A + U(g)]
or
"B has done nothing that can be   *pokala*
construed as *pokala*"   F [   ] ◄——— [   ]

then A in the first case cannot and in the second case will not allocate rights in the garden to B.

Thus the semantic relations among these propositions provide logical constraints on the allowable combinations of truth values of the propositions. These logical constraints make *inference* possible.

Inference

Inference is the process of determining the truth value of a proposition by bringing to bear on its possible truth values the constraints imposed by its relation to other propositions whose truth values have been previously determined. In some cases the relations are such that the truth value of one proposition is completely constrained by the truth values of other propositions. The inferences made under these conditions will be called *strong inferences*. Consider the schema below applied to events involving persons A and B.

$$
\begin{array}{ll}
\text{A} & \text{B} \\
[\text{R(g)}] &
\end{array}
$$

$$
\begin{array}{ccc}
& \textit{pokala} & \\
[\text{R(g)}] & \longleftarrow & [\quad] \\
& \text{R(g)} & \\
[\quad] & \longrightarrow & [\quad] \\
& & [\text{R(g)}]
\end{array}
$$

In the course of instantiating this schema, the following strong inferences are possible:

(1) The proposition $\begin{smallmatrix}\text{B}\\[\text{R(g)}]\end{smallmatrix}$ can be strongly inferred to be true if $[\overset{\text{A}}{\ }] \xrightarrow{\text{R(g)}} [\overset{\text{B}}{\ }]$ is true.

(2) The proposition $[\overset{\text{A}}{\ }] \xrightarrow{\text{R(g)}} [\overset{\text{B}}{\ }]$ can be strongly inferred to be false if either $\overset{\text{A}}{[\text{A(g)}]}$ or $[\overset{\text{A}}{\ }] \xleftarrow{\textit{pokala}} [\overset{\text{B}}{\ }]$ is false.

(3) Both $\begin{smallmatrix}\text{A}\\[\text{R(g)}]\end{smallmatrix}$ and $[\overset{\text{A}}{\ }] \xleftarrow{\textit{pokala}} [\overset{\text{B}}{\ }]$ can be strongly inferred to have been true if $[\overset{\text{A}}{\ }] \xrightarrow{\text{R(g)}} [\overset{\text{B}}{\ }]$ can be shown to be true.

(4) The proposition $[\overset{\text{A}}{\ }] \xrightarrow{\text{R(g)}} [\overset{\text{B}}{\ }]$ can be strongly inferred to be false if $\begin{smallmatrix}\text{B}\\[\text{R(g)}]\end{smallmatrix}$ has always been false.

For each of the strong inferences there is a corresponding inference in which the truth value of one proposition increases the likelihood that another proposition has a particular truth value. These inferences in which the truth value of a proposition is suggested by, but not determined by, the truth value of another proposition are called weak or *plausible inferences* (Polya, 1954). In these circumstances the semantic relations do not provide strong constraints.

(1) For example, what shall a reasoner do to his estimate of the likelihood that $[\overset{\text{A}}{\ }] \xrightarrow{\text{R(g)}} [\overset{\text{B}}{\ }]$ is true when it is learned that $\overset{\text{A}}{[\text{R(g)}]}$ and $[\overset{\text{A}}{\text{R(g)}}] \xleftarrow{\textit{pokala}} [\overset{\text{B}}{\ }]$ are both true? It is known that the joint truth of these two propositions does not cause the first proposition to be true because the rights holder may refuse to respond in the desired way. But knowing that A held rights in the garden makes him a possible allocator of rights, and knowing that

B provided *pokala* to A at least puts him in the running as a recipient. Thus, the likelihood that the allocation took place is increased by the knowledge that the enabling conditions have occurred. In the absence of information to the contrary, a reasoner may choose to "assume" that A has allocated rights to B. Such inferences are known in classical logic as fallacies, but they appear to play a major role in our everyday reasoning.

The other weak inferences are the following:

(2) Decrease the likelihood of $\begin{smallmatrix} B \\ [R(g)] \end{smallmatrix}$ if $\begin{smallmatrix} A \\ [\quad] \end{smallmatrix} \xrightarrow{R(g)} \begin{smallmatrix} B \\ [\quad] \end{smallmatrix}$ is false.

(3) Decrease the likelihood of either $\begin{smallmatrix} A \\ [R(g)] \end{smallmatrix}$ or

$\begin{smallmatrix} A \\ [\quad] \end{smallmatrix} \xleftarrow{pokala} \begin{smallmatrix} B \\ [\quad] \end{smallmatrix}$ if $\begin{smallmatrix} A \\ [\quad] \end{smallmatrix} \xrightarrow{R(g)} \begin{smallmatrix} B \\ [\quad] \end{smallmatrix}$ is false.

(4) Increase the likelihood of $\begin{smallmatrix} A \\ [\quad] \end{smallmatrix} \xrightarrow{R(g)} \begin{smallmatrix} B \\ [\quad] \end{smallmatrix}$ if $\begin{smallmatrix} B \\ [R(g)] \end{smallmatrix}$ is true.

When this notation is used to express the propositions that appear in actual discourse, the following conventions will be observed: Each proposition that has been inferred will appear with its inferred truth value either before or after the proposition. When the truth value has been determined via a strong inference, the truth value shown will be preceded by a lower-case letter s; for example, s.T indicates a proposition that has been inferred to be true through a strong inference. When the truth value was arrived at via a weak inference, the truth value shown will be preceded by a lower-case letter p; for example, p.F indicates a proposition that is plausibly inferred to be false.

While it is possible to use such a network of logical relations to infer the truth value of a proposition from an inferred truth value of another, the chain of inference must ultimately be anchored by a proposition whose truth value is established by observation, or lacking that, by social convention. Of the propositions that make up the schema, some are more easily assigned truth values by observation than others. Since there are no observable marks on either men or units of land to indicate that a relation obtains between them, the truth values of propositions representing rights in land can only be established through inference. In addition to relations within the schema, the individual propositions of the schema have relations to other propositions outside. Some of these relations might be thought of as scripts for the internal structure of the propositions.[2] Thus, for example, there is script-like knowledge about the typical actions of a man who has use rights in a piece of land. A holder of use rights usually either gardens the plot himself or has someone garden it for him each time the major field in which it is located is gardened by the community. On the strength of this script-like knowledge, the fact that a man has not gardened a plot of land himself nor had someone garden it for him may be taken as circumstantial evidence against an assertion of his having use rights in the garden.

The inferences required to establish the truth values of propositions about rights in land will necessarily involve propositions about *pokala* and allocations of rights. These are observable events, the truth values of which can sometimes be established directly by observation. In the context of litigation, the veracity of observations may be supported by the testimony of witnesses. While a single observation is sometimes sufficient to establish that such an event has occurred, it is often the case that no practical number of discrete observations can establish that a specific event has not occurred. In such cases one cannot rule out the possibility that the event sought occurred when one was not looking. Because of the differences in observability of the propositions, some of the inferences available in the schema are made more frequently and more naturally than others. The most common inferences are the first two of the strong inferences and the first two of the weak inferences. The first of the strong inferences is usually combined with the first of the weak inferences to form an episode in which all of the constituent propositions are true. Such an episode would typically be used to support one's own claims to rights in land. The second of the strong inferences combines with the second of the weak inferences to form an episode in which all of the constituent propositions are false. This would be used in the refutation of someone else's claim to rights in land.

Descendant Schemata

(1) The first of the descendant schemata follows more or less trivially from the principle that within the "owning" *dala* all available rights in a particular piece of land will be transferred intact. Thus, the prototypic *pokala* within the *dala* resulting in a transfer of both rights of allocation and use rights looks like this:

$$A$$
$$[A + U(g)]$$

$$[A + U(g)] \quad \overset{pokala}{\longleftarrow} \quad B \quad [\quad\quad]$$

$$[\quad] \xrightarrow{\text{A}+\text{U(g)}} [\quad]$$

$$[\text{A}+\text{U(g)}]$$

(2) When the *pokala* is between rather than within a *dala,* the right of allocation over the garden cannot be transferred out of the owning *dala.* The title in the garden, therefore, becomes split between the two *dala*:

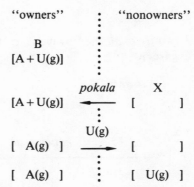

(3) *Pokala* within a *dala* results in the transfer of all available rights, but as a result of the use rights having gone out to a "nonowning" *dala,* all that remains within the *dala* is the right of allocation.

$$\begin{array}{c}\text{B}\\ [\ \text{A(g)}\ ]\end{array}$$

$$[\quad] \xrightarrow[\ ]{\substack{\text{C} \qquad\qquad \textit{pokala}}} [\ \text{A(g)}\ ]$$

$$[\quad] \xleftarrow{\text{A(g)}} [\quad]$$

$$[\ \text{A(g)}\ ]$$

(4) *Katumamata*—or waking up a previous *pokala* between *dala*—differs from schema 2, *pokala* between *dala,* only in that the use rights to the garden have already gone out of the "owning" *dala.* The further payment of *katumamata* enables the allocation of those use rights to another member of the "nonowning" *dala.* The rights will remain with him until his death.

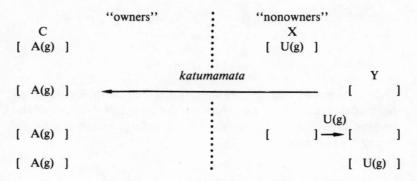

(5) In *katuyumali* the "owners" of the garden regain use rights in their garden.

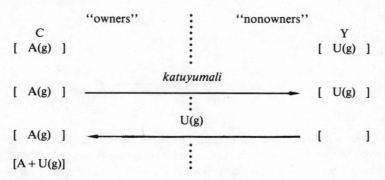

(6) In the last descendant schema to be discussed, the headman by default takes rights remaining after the settlement of an estate. This schema is not a true descendant of the master schema because it does not involve any social reciprocation, yet it is necessary to the operation of the system.

$$\not{C}$$
$$[A + U(g)]$$
Headman

$$\xrightarrow{A + U(g)} \quad [\quad]$$

$$[A + U(g)]$$

I have arranged these schemata here such that they could be concatenated in order to form a single history of a particular garden. The terminal states of some of them match the entry states of others. Where this is the case, the events represented could sensibly follow each other. The fact that the terminal and entry states are not the same in all of the schemata means that there are sequences of events that could not sensibly occur. It makes no sense, for instance, that a transfer of use rights within the owning *dala* immediately follows a successful *katumamata* episode.

I consider these schemata to be components of a cultural grammar or code of the discourse about relations among men and land. The minimal viable unit in discourse is not the sentence but a set of propositions which encode an episode, that is, a set which describes, however incompletely, a transfer of rights in land from one person to another. The schemata provide a specification of the organization of relations among the component propositions. An ungrammatical organization lacks sensibility; it is not culturally meaningful. That is not to say that a sensible organization is necessarily true. Just as grammatical sentences may represent propositions which are false, meaningful arguments may come to false conclusions. A compelling deception is one that makes perfect sense. It is a common and sometimes dangerous folk strategy to treat sensibility as an indication of truthfulness. Such a heuristic is understandable, though, in light of the comparative ease of judging sensibility versus judging truth in most discourse. The importance of schemata such as these is that they are the standards by which sensibility is judged.

4 | Case Analysis

I N THE MONTHS of July and August of 1976 I recorded three cases of land litigation before the Tukwaukwa village court (Fig. 6). In the course of developing the ethnography of land tenure and the model of land transfer schemata, all three cases were taken into account. One involved an instance of *wokosi,* the dying out of a *dala* line and the confusion of titles that resulted when three other *dala* made claims to the extinct *dala's* land. A second case arose between maternal half brothers as a result of their mother's changing husbands, hamlets, and instructions for the allocation of her land. A third case, the simplest and most straightforward of the three, involved a misinterpretation of an event in the history of a garden. This case is reported below. It was chosen over the others for presentation here because it illustrates the necessary points with a minimal cast of characters and a relatively uncomplicated history of events.

The case of Kailimila versus Motabasi was heard before the Tukwaukwa village court on July 26, 1976. The garden in dispute, named Kuluboku, is not in the Tukwaukwa garden lands but on the border between major garden fields (*kwabila*) of neighboring villages Teyava and Oyveyova (see Fig. 7). Kailimila is a resident of Teyava village. Motabasi has resided in Tukwaukwa, then Teyava, then Port Moresby (the national capital), and now lives in a splinter hamlet of Tukwaukwa called Luvaka. The case was brought to Tukwaukwa because both men have considerable power and there is no authority in the small village of Teyava sufficient to make a decision stick. As we shall see, however, even the authority of the high ranking *guyau* of Tukwaukwa is challenged by the losing litigant.

Kailimila and Motabasi are matrilineal parallel cousins (*tuwa/ bwada*), older and younger brother in the Kiriwinian reckoning (see Fig. 8). The case arose when Motabasi, assuming that the garden

Figure 6. *A scene from Trobriand land litigation; the author makes a stereophonic tape recording of the proceedings while a litigant states his claim and villagers listen*

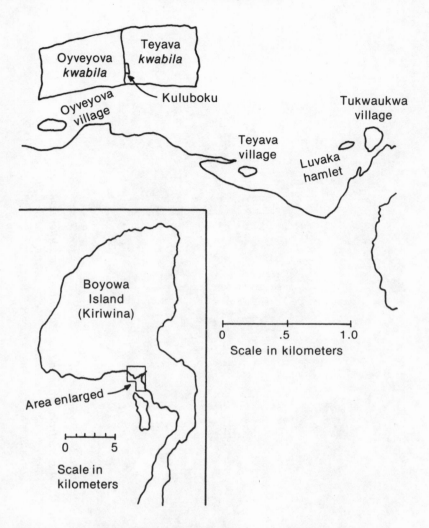

Figure 7. *Map of Kulumata district of Boyowa Island*

was under his control, sent a younger man, Modalewa, to cut it. The relation between Motabasi and Modalewa is not specified in the proceedings and is not crucial to the decision. From other information it seems most likely to have been a *kaikeda* arrangement (see Chapter 2). Kailimila, hearing that Modalewa was cutting the garden which he himself intended to cut, brought the matter to court.

Since it is exceedingly difficult to follow the litigant's arguments without substantial prior knowledge about the events referred to, I will present here a synopsis of the events which are relevant to the disposition of the garden in question. This is my version of the se-

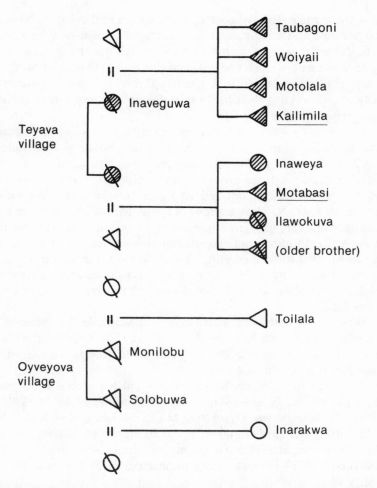

Darkened entries indicate members of the owning subclan (*dala*)

Figure 8. *Partial genealogy for the case of Kailimila* v. *Motabasi*

quence of events most likely underlying the litigation observed. In assembling it I considered the text of the litigation itself as well as the commentary of other informants both before and after the court proceedings. Since the participants in the case fail to agree on what actually happened, the account presented here may not in fact represent the absolute truth with regard to the history of the garden.

Neither litigant traces the history of the garden plot Kuluboku further back than to an unnamed older brother of Motabasi. This man held use rights and the right of allocation to the garden. Motabasi once joined the crewmen of the older brother's canoe in cutting the garden. This, of course, is not an unusual event: to have a large canoe and a permanent crew is the mark of a wealthy man. The potential heirs of such a man might well use the cutting of a garden as an opportunity to *pokala* the old man. This older brother died, giving the garden to his sister, Ilawokuva, who resided in Teyava. Ilawokuva then held the rights to Kuluboku for several gardening seasons.

Solobuwa, an important man in nearby Oyveyova village, gave *pokala* to Ilawokuva for the garden plot Kuluboku. Since the plot lay at the boundary of the Teyava and Oyveyova *kwabila,* it was easy to build the fence around it and include it in the Oyveyova enclosure. Ilawokuva allocated use rights to Solobuwa in response to his *pokala.* Solobuwa grew old and Monilobu, Solobuwa's younger brother, brought *katumamata* of one arm of bananas to Ilawokuva. Motabasi was apparently visiting Teyava at the time and witnessed the presentation. Thinking the presentation was an initial *pokala* rather than *katumamata* for Solobuwa's previous *pokala,* Motabasi advised Ilawokuva not to give the garden to Monilobu.

In Motabasi's absence, Ilawokuva told Kailimila that when the elderly Solobuwa died, Kailimila should retrieve the garden Kuluboku. Kailimila will later claim in court that Ilawokuva told him nothing of Monilobu's *katumamata*.

Solobuwa died. When the *kwabila* in which Kuluboku lies was next cut by the Teyava villagers Kailimila went out to cut Kuluboku. In neighboring Oyveyova, Monilobu heard that Kailimila was cutting the garden and went out to stop him. Kailimila and Monilobu fought in the garden and in the village. A court was convened in Tukwaukwa village to hear the case. This was about thirty years ago.

Monilobu won the case and took use rights to the garden. The right of allocation was acknowledged to be Kailimila's. Kailimila was instructed by the court to find what wealth he could and *katuyumali* to Monilobu in order to return the garden to his *dala*. Kailimila presented *katuyumali* to Monilobu, and recovered the use rights to Kuluboku. He began gardening Kuluboku.

Up until this time, Motabasi had been living in Tukwaukwa and gardening for Inaveguwa, his mother's sister. At this point he moved to Teyava and began gardening for Ilawokuva, his sister. Motabasi gardened for Ilawokuva for about fifteen years. In response, she gave him the rights to three gardens. Kuluboku was not among the three.

Meanwhile, Kailimila was *tolibaleku* of Kuluboku and gardened it three times (in three nonconsecutive seasons) by himself. Motabasi went to Port Moresby to work as a laborer in a government project. In a fourth season, which came while Motabasi was in Port Moresby, Kailimila had two other men, Mekuvi and Kwemwai, garden Kuluboku for him. Motabasi returned from Port Moresby after an absence of several years and took up residence in the Tu-kwaukwa hamlet of Luvaka.

At the beginning of the 1976-77 gardening season, Motabasi sent Modalewa to garden the plot Kuluboku. Kailimila and his brothers heard about Modalewa cutting the garden. They told Motabasi it was not his right to garden that land and brought the case to court.

Motabasi's Presentation

The texts which follow are translations of original transcripts in the Trobriand language. All analysis is performed on the original transcripts. The translation is *not* a part of the analytic process, but is provided only to allow the reader access to the material.

In the first segment of the court transcript, the litigants are joined by Tovalugwa, a village Local Government Council member, who is acting as bailiff in the case. The case opens with Motabasi protesting that he is unprepared to dispute because he has been given no warning that a case was brought against him. He pleads that the case be delayed until his witnesses can arrive from Teyava and Oyveyova. The *guyau,* Murebodema, decides that the litigants should make their presentations anyway because many villagers are anxious to get out to their own gardens to work. Murebodema declares that no decision will be made regarding the disposition of the garden until Motabasi's witnesses arrive and give their testimony.

The case proper begins with the bailiff, Tovalugwa, instructing the litigants.

TOVALUGWA:
1. The garden is yours (pl).
2. However, you shall give evidence in an orderly fashion regarding who took it, who held it, who gave it to whom, and who has gardened it.
3. You shall not argue heatedly, you shall not disturb the village, you shall not fight.
4. This is your (pl) garden.
5. You shall argue only who has the right to hold it and look after it.
6. You, Kailimila. You have been cutting the garden yet today Motabasi touches it.
7. Motabasi. Whatever is your understanding of this garden which your companion (Kailimila) held and cut that you went and cut it, as if to garden? Report it now that we might understand and your companion might understand.

MOTABASI:

8. Ask him (Kailimila) where he got this plot which he held and gardened.
9. He summoned me (to court), so let him speak.

TOVALUGWA:

10. Kailimila, Motabasi wonders where you got this garden.

KAILIMILA:

11. I should speak first?

TOVALUGWA:

12. Good, you speak first.

KAILIMILA:

13. I think he should go first.
14. Because he grabbed it from my hand, you should hear his way first.
15. Since I already held it, I should speak after, right?

TOVALUGWA:

16. Yes, that is right.
17. Since you have already been cutting it.
18. Motabasi bends over (to hold it) so fine, let him speak first.

MOTABASI:

19. O.K. I will speak first because I don't have any witnesses.
20. It is not Motolala's garden, nor Woiyaii's, nor Taubagoni's.
21. It is easy for me to take up this garden and cut it.
22. I was cutting it when my younger brothers said,
23. "You have recently come."
24. "You shall not touch these things."
25. "These are our (ex. pl.) things because we *pokala*'ed previously."
26. But as you know this was a woman's garden.
27. Ilawokuvamalasi's garden.
28. My older brother cut it by himself.
29. (When) he died, he gave it to his sister.
30. I thought I had finished the talk of Wawawa, but that is not so.
31. Monumoiya and Tosunaiya cut it for the old man.
32. Therefore I came to reside in Teyava and saw my sister at a different veranda (living apart from her kinspeople).
33. I had worked hard with them, for our mother (Inaveguwa).
34. But because my sister had no one, I said to myself,

35. "O, this is not good. I will do a bit of *kaivatam* of course."
36. People of Tukwaukwa I eat your excrement, compared to your gardens the one I made for her was so small.
37. It met her needs, so to speak.
38. I held Wawawa.
39. I held Kapwalelamauna, where today I garden Bodawiya's small yams.
40. I held Bwesakau.
41. I held Kuluboku.
42. I know that Monilobu on his own gave one arm of bananas to my sister.
43. She said, "Come and eat this arm of bananas the old man's *pokala*."
44. I said, "Who?"
45. "Monilobu thinks it has already gone inside his fence, he wants that garden."
46. I said, "O sister, land is very dear. Let him bring a bit more."
47. Well, a while back I went to Moresby.
48. He, of course, cut it that time I was in Moresby.
49. Mokaibwai said, "Go to your garden. It is no good that you disappear and he cuts it."
50. Today I touch it, Modalewa will cut it.
51. Because I have not touched that garden at all, truly I have not touched it.
52. That one time we cut it, all of his canoe crewmen went and cut it.
53. I say this, Inaweya, Idulisa, tell them.
54. This thing has been lying in my ear.
55. My sister gave it into my hand.
56. My younger brothers have not supported their sister.
57. They supported their mother.
58. I went and we supported their mother.
59. If I had taken their mother's garden, o I would give them their thing.
60. But because of that woman, Ilawokuvamalasi, it is mine alone.
61. The Teyava people will say the same thing when they come.
62. That is all.

TOVALUGWA:

63. Motabasi, I ask you, you went, you worked with your friends, you came back here.
64. How many years did you cut this garden anew, or to whom did you give it to cut?

MOTABASI:

65. They have not touched it, it has simply stood until today.
66. Hey, from the time he (Kailimila) cut it until the present it has just stood there.

TOVALUGWA:

67. They have not cut it even once more?

MOTABASI:

68. They have not cut it even once more.

TOVALUGWA:

69. From when you began when he cut it until the present? It has simply stood and today they will cut it?

MOTABASI:

70. Yes, it has stood and today they will cut it.

TOVALUGWA:

71. O.K.

Analysis of Motabasi's Presentation

The principles of land tenure are a sort of knowledge structure which describes the workings of a small but important segment of Trobriand experience. This knowledge structure by itself is not sufficient to account for all of the organization of Motabasi's presentation, but it does account for that portion of the discourse which deals directly with the issues of the transfers of rights in land.

It is assumed that such a knowledge structure can be employed in at least two ways. If attributed to a speaker, the knowledge structure is capable of participation in the generation of discourse. That is, the knowledge structure, or something like it, is used by the speaker in organizing what he says. On the other hand, the knowledge structure is also used by those who are listening to a speaker to interpret and evaluate what the speaker says. The knowledge structure is assumed to be a cognitive structure which is shared by the participants to the litigation. Such a structure, then, performs different cognitive functions depending on the requirements of the task.

The role of the knowledge structure in the organization of discourse will be demonstrated by showing that the propositions in discourse are instantiations of the component relations of the transfer schemata.

Statements 1-19 deal with the details of court procedure, and although they are interesting in their own right, they do not directly address the issues of rights to land. The verbal parrying that goes on here relies on the notion that it is a disadvantage to make the first presentation in court because it gives the opponent an opportunity to counter each of one's claims.

EPISODE 1

Motabasi's opening statements are a set of assertions which set up the problem with which he will have to deal in his argument. In statement 20, Motabasi lists the names of his younger brothers and denies that it is their garden.

20. *Gala bilekula Motolala, gala bilekula Woiyaii, gala bilekula Taubagoni.* It is not Motolala's garden, nor Woiyaii's, nor Taubagoni's.
21. *Igagabila bakalakova kaina balitaki.* It is easy for me to take up this garden and cut it.
22. *Balitaki, balitaki, igau deli bwadagwa ikaibigasi,* I was cutting it when my younger brothers said,
23. *"Yokwa makateki lokuma."* "You have recently come."

In statements 21 and 22, Motabasi speaks in the first person of cutting the garden. This is figurative in two ways. First, cutting the garden, the first major step in the individual garden cycle, is a synecdoche for the conduct of the entire garden cycle. This figure of speech will be observed throughout the litigation. Second, Motabasi himself is not doing the gardening. He has delegated the actual gardening work to Modalewa, one of his followers.

24. *"Gala bukukwabukwani makwesina vavagi."* "You shall not touch these things."
25. *"Mavavagisa pela bogwa kapokalabogwasi."* "These are our (ex. pl.) things because we *pokala*'ed previously."

Motabasi reports his brothers' claim (in SS24-25) that they have already *pokala*'ed for this garden. While it was Kailimila who actually presented the *pokala* and was given rights in the garden plot, his younger brothers very likely helped him with the *pokala* payment and were probably going to do the actual gardening of the plot for Kailimila. The conceptual representations of the propositions of this episode are given in Table 1. In order to win the case, Motabasi will have to support or defend the propositions of statements 20 and 21, and he will have to reject or refute the propositions of statements 24 and 25. Statement 25 is an explicit reference

Table 1   Motabasi's first episode of discourse

Motolala	Woiyaii	Taubagoni
F [A + U(Kb)] 20	F [A + U(Kb)] 20	F [A + U(Kb)] 20

Motabasi
[A + U(Kb)] 21

Motabasi
F [A + U(Kb)] 23, 24

?
[A + U(Kb)]

pokala   Bros.
[A + U(Kb)]   ◄——— [   ] 25

A + U(Kb)
[   ] ———► [   ]

[A + U(Kb)] 25

to the results of a transfer of rights in land, yet it is incompletely specified in two ways. First, it does not specify all of the participants in the events mentioned, and second, it does not even mention all of the events involved. There is no way to recover a specification of the unmentioned participants from such a description, but unstated events can be recovered by determining which schema is invoked by the propositions that do appear. The first problem for a processor is the choice of an appropriate knowledge structure. In this analysis, that means the choice of a schema on which to model events.

Motabasi knows that his brothers are, like himself, "owners" of Kuluboku. He assumes that Ilawokuva (also an "owner") has held the garden. The circumstance his brothers describe is, therefore, an instance of *pokala* and transfer inside the owning *dala*.

Motabasi is thus able to infer from his brother's statement that his brothers believe that someone else held the garden and that as a result of their *pokala* the rights holder allocated the garden to them. The fact that Motabasi is unable to specify to whom the brothers claim to have *pokala*'ed will be important later in the case. Much of his presentation will be attempts to block possible claims by Kailimila with respect to the people Motabasi believes most likely to have been the recipients of the brothers' *pokala*.

Having defined the problem with these opening assertions, Motabasi moves on to an account of the history of rights in the garden. In making the transition from his brothers' claim, which he considers to be counterfactual, to his own assertions about the history of the garden, he uses the propositional disjunction *mitaga* which can be glossed "but" or "however."

EPISODE 2

26. *Mitaga bogwa kunukwalisa baleku bilekuvivila.* But as you know this was a woman's garden.
27. *Ilawokuvamalasi la baleku.* Ilawokuvamalasi's garden.
28. *Itatai kalamwaguta tuwagu.* My older brother cut it by himself.
29. *Ikaliga, luleta isimakava wala.* (When) he died, he gave it to his sister.

This transaction is shown in Table 2. It is not surprising that the proposition describing the actual *pokala* remains unarticulated. Since this is a garden passing to a woman, from a wealthy older brother, it is unlikely that any memorable formal *pokala* was actually involved (see Chapter 2). As we shall see later, this particular transfer of rights is not only unchallenged, it is essential to the opponent's argument as well.

In the third unit, Motabasi continues to trace the history of the garden, establishing his own relation to it.

EPISODE 3

32. *Mapela avilobusi Teyava agisi luguta ituwali la kaukweda.* Therefore I came to reside in Teyava and saw my sister at a different veranda (living apart from her kinspeople).
33. *Yegu atota peula besa matosina, pela inamasi.* I had worked hard with them, for our mother (Inaveguwa).
34. *E, mitaga pela luguta gala tetala, kawagu,* But because my sister had no one, I said to myself,

Table 2 Motabasi's second unit of discourse

Older brother
$[A + U(Kb)]$ 28

	pokala	Ilawokuva	
$[A + U(Kb)]$	◄——	[	] unspecified, but inferrable

	$A + U(Kb)$		
[	] ——►	[	] 29

$[A + U(Kb)]$ 27

---

35. *"O, gala bwena. Bavagi pikekita kaivatamla gola."* "O, this is not good. I will do a bit of *kaivatam* of course."
36. *Akoma pwami kumwedomi Tukwaukwa, makala mi bagula, pikekita wala lavagi pela minana tomota.* People of Tukwaukwa I eat your excrement, compared to your gardens the one I made for her was so small.
37. *Katubodala kalabiga.* It met her needs, so to speak.
38. *Wawawa ayosi.* I held Wawawa.
39. *Kapwalelamauna ayosi, makwena lagela Bodawiya kala bwanawa.* I held Kapwalelamauna, where today I garden Bodawiya's small yams.
40. *Bwesakau ayosi.* I held Bwesakau.
41. *Kuluboku ayosi.* I held Kuluboku.

In context it is a very responsible act for Motabasi to take on the gardening for a female kinsperson who has no one else to garden for her.

Statement 36 is, of course, a rhetorical understatement. Motabasi neither eats excrement, nor did he make an especially small garden for his sister, but in saying so he compliments the people of Tukwaukwa who are hearing his case.

The garden plots named in statements 38-41 are those which Motabasi claims were given to him by Ilawokuva. In statement 39 he again points out how responsible he is by mentioning his current gardening for another kinswoman.

The previous unit supported the assertion that Ilawokuva held Kuluboku. Taking that as the starting point for this unit, the application of the schema 1 generates the organization shown in Table 3. In this interpretation, Motabasi's rights in Kuluboku are made credible but are not proved. If statements 27 and 35 are true, then they do not entail, but they make credible, Ilawokuva's (unstated) allocation of rights to Motabasi. Since her allocation and his acquisition of rights are linked by causality, his rights become as credible as her allocation. Notice that to this point Motabasi has not made any strong inferences. He has simply stated a credibly connected set of conditions in support of his case.

EPISODE 4

In the fourth episode, Motabasi deals with the first of several anticipated threats to his claim.

42. *Anukwali wala kalamwaguta Monilobu kaitala usi iseki luguta.* I know that Monilobu on his own gave one arm of bananas to my sister.

Table 3 Motabasi's third unit of discourse

Ilawokuva
[A + U(Wa,Kap,Bwe,Kb)]

$$\underset{kaivatam}{\overset{pokala}{[A + U(Wa,Kap,Bwe,Kb)] \quad \longleftarrow \quad}} \text{Motabasi} \quad [\quad\quad] 35\text{-}36$$

$$\overset{A + U(Wa,Kap,Bwe,Kb)}{[\quad\quad\quad] \quad \longrightarrow \quad} [\quad\quad] \text{ presupposed by other statements}$$

[A + U(Wa)] 38

[A + U(Kap)] 39

[A + U(Bwe)] 40

[A + U(Kb)] 41

43. *Ikaibiga, "So, makaina usi kukomasi la pokala tomwaiya."* She said, "Come and eat this arm of bananas, the old man's *pokala*."
44. *Kawagu, "Avela?"* I said, "Who?"
45. *"Monilobu idoki bogwa kidamwa lela okala kali, magila baleku makwena."* "Monilobu thinks it has already gone inside his fence, he wants that garden."
46. *Kawagu, "O luguta, pwaipwaiya sena mwau. Igau sitana tuvela."* I said, "O sister, land is very dear. Let him bring a bit more."

In statements 43-46 Motabasi describes a conversation he had with Ilawokuva about Monilobu's *pokala*. He does not state what Ilawokuva's decision was, but he indicates that he told her the *pokala* was insufficient. If she took his advice (and I believe that in his presentation he wanted the listeners to make that conversational inference) that would yield the set of propositions shown in Table 4.

It is a common presentation device in Trobriand discourse to report entire conversations. Motabasi's recollection of the conversation reveals that he thought the bananas brought by Monilobu were *pokala* rather than *katumamata*. This is quite reasonable because Motabasi was living in Tukwaukwa at the time of Solobuwa's original *pokala*. If Monilobu's prestation had been *pokala*, one arm of bananas would have been quite insufficient and Motabasi would have been correct in advising his sister to hold out for more

Table 4   Motabasi's fourth unit of discourse

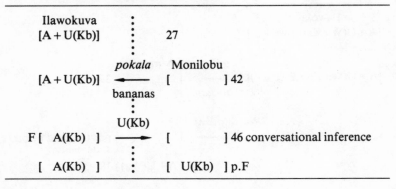

pokala. For a *katumamata,* however, it was sufficient. Motabasi's interpretation of this event will be crucial to the outcome of the case.

Since Monilobu is not a member of the owning *dala,* the headman schema (schema 6) and the *katuyumali* schema (schema 5) cannot be applicable. The *katumamata* schema (schema 4), which we know to be the correct model of these events, is not considered by Motabasi because he believed that Ilawokuva was holding use rights in Kuluboku at the time of the presentation. Given that, the schema above is seen by the litigant Motabasi to be the only appropriate model of the events cited. Once the truth value of the proposition "Ilawokuva allocates use rights in Kuluboku to Monilobu" is established as false, the only culturally meaningful interpretation is one in which the proposition "Monilobu has use rights in Kuluboku" is also false. Motabasi does not at this point in his presentation state the plausible inference product: "Monilobu has no rights in Kuluboku," although it is implicit in his presentation. At a later point in the litigation, however, Motabasi argues that Monilobu died before bringing sufficient *pokala* and therefore could not have held the garden.

EPISODE 5

Motabasi then returns to his statement that his sister gave the garden to him.

54. *Makwenaga bogwa otaigagu ikanabogwa.* This thing has been lying in my ear.
55. *Luguta isakaigu o yamagu.* My sister gave it into my hand.

What has been lying in his ear is his sister's declaration that Motabasi should take the gardens. This is a reiteration of his second unit of discourse and appears in Table 5.

Table 5   Motabasi's fifth unit of discourse

Ilawokuva
[A + U(Kb)] 27

	pokala	Motabasi	
[A + U(Kb)]	◄———	[	] 36

	A + U(Kb)		
[ ]	———►	[	] 55

[A + U(Kb)] p.T

EPISODE 6

In the sixth unit, Motabasi dismisses a threat from his younger brothers (see Table 6).

56. *Bwadagwa gala ipeulasi besa lusita*. My younger brothers have not supported their sister.

Motabasi can legitimately infer that Ilawokuva did not allocate rights in Kuluboku to Motabasi's younger brothers. From that he cannot actually infer that they have not legitimately gained rights to the garden. But in the absence of another model of the events (and he seems aware of none) and in light of his own claims, his brothers' lack of rights in Kuluboku is rendered credible.

EPISODE 7

Motabasi's seventh unit of discourse is a counterfactual one which he will construct and then refute. In contrast to statement 56, Motabasi offers statement 57.

Table 6   Motabasi's sixth unit of discourse

Ilawokuva
[A + U(g)]

	pokala	Bros.	
F [A + U(g)]	◄———	[	] 56

	A + U(g)		
[ ]	———►	[	] s.F

[A + U(g)] p.F

57. *Ipeulasi besa inasi.* They supported their mother.
58. *Lawa kapeulasi besa inasi.* I went and we supported their mother.
59. *Kidamwa bilekula inasi bakau, o baseki si vavagi.* If I had taken their mother's garden, o I would give them their thing.

The propositions in statement 59 are, of course, connected through the organization provided by schema 1 on the left in Table 7.

In this episode, Motabasi has hypothetically varied the premises. He poses the question "What if Inaveguwa was *tolibaleku* of Kuluboku?" and answers that were that the case he would give the garden to his brothers. Motabasi is wrestling with a difficult problem here. In statement 25 he was unable to specify to whom the brothers claimed to have *pokala*'ed to receive the garden. We know from other sources that they actually gave *pokala* in the form of *katuyumali* to Monilobu. This event is, however, apparently outside Motabasi's horizon of awareness. He does not know to whom they *pokala*'ed, so to cover himself, he attempts to reject claims which might be made with respect to either of the two most likely sources of the garden. The disadvantage at which Motabasi stands by virtue of having to go first in court is clear here. Had Kailimila given his version first, it probably would not have changed the outcome of the case, but Motabasi very likely would have constructed his arguments in a more focused way if he had known in advance to whom his brothers claim to have given *pokala*. In episode 6 he attempted to show that his brothers did not receive the garden by giving *pokala* to Ilawokuva. In this unit, he says that if his brothers think they got the garden by giving *pokala* to Inaveguwa, that is fine, but it is hypothetical. Again, marking the disjunction between what he sees as hypothetical and what he sees as factual with the propositional conjunction *mitaga,* he moves to refute episode seven.

EPISODE 8

60. *Mitaga pela vivila minana, Ilawokuvamalasi, agumwaguta wala.* But because of that woman, Ilawokuvamalasi, it is mine alone.

For the phrase "because of the woman, Ilawokuva" we can read what he has earlier asserted and derived about his relation to her and to the garden Kuluboku. Thus, we construct episode 8 as shown in Table 8. Having now reached the end of his presentation, Motabasi has explicitly instantiated all of the relations in the schema. He has done so in a way that makes his claims to the garden credible.

Table 7 Motabasi's seventh and ninth units of discourse

Ina [A + U(Kb)] 59—hypothetical	Ina F [A + U(Kb)]
pokala Bros. [A + U(Kb)] ◄——— [ ] 57	*pokala* Bros. [A + U(Kb)] ◄——— [ ]
A + U(Kb) [ ] ———► [ ] p.T s.F [	A + U(Kb)] ———► [ ]
[A + U(Kb)] p.T	p.F [A + U(Kb)]

Table 8 Motabasi's eighth unit of discourse

Ilawokuva
[A + U(Kb)] 27

pokala   Motabasi
[A + U(Kb)] ◄——— [   ] 36

A + U(Kb)
[   ] ———► [   ] 55

[A + U(Kb)] 60

The refutation of the hypothetical episode 7 is implicit in episode 8. For the period of time in question, Ilawokuva is believed by Motabasi to be holding the rights to Kuluboku. That means that Inaveguwa is not holding the rights to Kuluboku. Plugging that into the structure shown in episode 7, the entire set of propositions can be reinterpreted as shown in the right column of Table 7. This shadow interpretation defeats the hypothetical interpretation presented in episode 7 (left column of Table 7). If the younger brothers think they control the garden by virtue of their *pokala* to their mother, then they are mistaken. Later in his presentations, Motabasi stresses that Inaveguwa never held the garden Kuluboku.

Here, at the end of his first presentation to the court, Motabasi has not proved that none of his younger brothers has rights to Kuluboku. As we shall see, the court will decide that it is Kailimila and not Motabasi who has rights to the garden. Motabasi has, however, demonstrated that his own claims to the garden are credible, that is, they conform to the organization of the knowledge structure which defines the nature of transfers of rights in land. He has also shown that none of his brothers came to hold rights in

Kuluboku by getting them from what appear to Motabasi as the two most likely sources. Thus, Motabasi's presentation is credible but not truly compelling. He has given a reasonable account of his own relations to the garden, but he has not successfully refuted the claims of his brothers.

Kailimila's Presentation

Immediately following the completion of Motabasi's presentation, Tovalugwa instructed Kailimila to give his version.

KAILIMILA:

77. (That was) His road, therefore I think I will speak that road as well.
78. (It is) Not Motolala, not Woiyaii, not Taubagoni, not Inaveguwa.
79. He (Motabasi) was still in Tukwaukwa, later he would show up in Teyava, (but this is when he was) still in Tukwaukwa.
80. I was still a young bachelor myself.
81. I was a bachelor, but not a bachelor without responsibility.
82. I was already gardening and becoming a man, so to speak.
83. I was gardening, she (Ilawokuva) simply said,
84. "You remember that (garden at) our fence (Kuluboku)."
85. "Our kinsmen have come and taken it away, but you remember it."
86. "When Solobuwa dies, you go get it."
87. Well, she might have told me something like,
88. "You think a bit about the younger man there, Monilobu."
89. She might have told me and I could have done it in a more peaceful way.
90. But she did not tell me anything like that.
91. Ringworm man (Solobuwa suffered from ringworm) died, as they say, and I went out to cut the garden.
92. I went out to cut it and Monilobu heard about it.
93. We came to grips in the forest.
94. We finished our fight in the forest . . .
95. Perhaps you(pl.) were just children, or perhaps Sibwekewa (an old man listening to the case) know something of it.
96. It was in Tukwaukwa that Monilobu and I went to court, Tukwaukwa and nowhere else.
97. Kolosi and Kagumasima were the police, Kuradoga the counselor.
98. We had argued as if it was a fist fight, so to speak.
99. The police and counselor stood back, so to speak, and cut the case.

100. They said,
101. "Don't make it a fight."
102. "Kailimila, you remember, this thing has already gone to Oyveyova."
103. "It has gone to Oyveyova, the old men (Solobuwa and Monilobu) already hold it."
104. "Now you(pl.) have finished the court proceedings, the old man (Monilobu) holds it."
105. "Now, you remember and go to your village."
106. "Go get whatever you can to recover your thing (the garden)."
107. So, I laid down four ceremonial yams, two arms of bananas, two bunches of betel nut, and a small clay pot.
108. This I took to the old man, Monilobu.
109. (He said,) "Your thing goes to you."
110. A while back Motabasi gardened for Inaveguwa.
111. He gardened for our(exc.pl.) mother.
112. Because I had already begun this *kaivatam*, so to speak.
113. He didn't go to me (and say),
114. "I think I will cut a big garden for myself (that is, use Kuluboku)."
115. I would have heard if he had.
116. He never prepared that garden.
117. He went, perhaps he recently went and took the garden first, or perhaps he took the garden first and then came, he went to Teyava.
118. I don't know, I have forgotten, as they say.
119. He can explain.
120. He didn't (garden it) one day, he told you, not one day.
121. Myself, I cut it once, I cut it twice, I cut it thrice.
122. Tolukuyabi made a *kaiyasa*, Tolukuyabi had a big *kaiyasa*, as you know, with Togewasi, then I cut it the third time.
123. The fourth time Kwemwai and Mekuvi did a bit, but mostly it lay fallow.
124. It stands there at the end.
125. And today I will garden it because I know what is mine.
126. The Malasi people gave it to me first.
127. He went and gardened for Inaveguwa.
128. Yes, he did as he has told you, as he told us.
129. He did a bit of *kaivatam* for the old woman (Ilawokuva).
130. She allocated his gardens as you have heard, Wawawa, Kapwalelamauna, and Bwesakau.
131. Those three are his gardens.
132. He cuts them (regularly).
133. Is that nothing? Should I rise up and cut them?

134. What for?
135. (As if to himself,) The woman gave them to me, (saying) "Come and cut them."
136. No! I have not touched them.
137. They are his things. (Motabasi protests in background)
138. The Malasi people gave him his things.
139. I have just one thing that they have given me.
140. Not a second, nor a third, lord knows there is only one.

MOTABASI:
141. Call Inaweya to come.
142. I supported Inaweya.

KAILIMILA:
143. My road ends here.
144. The Malasi people gave him his gardens and they gave me this single one.

MOTABASI:
145. We stand here, we speak of gardens, yet we refuse our witnesses.

KAILIMILA:
146. I went and brought it back from the hand of Monilobu.
147. I have already said this.
148. Now he (Motabasi) would spoil our(exc.dual) way by snatching it from my hand.
149. As if he would turn things around.
150. That's all.

Analysis of Kailimila's Presentation

Kailimila begins his presentation by ridiculing Motabasi's. In statements 77 and 78, he repeats Motabasi's phrasing and adds Inaveguwa's name to the list of people who do not hold Kuluboku. As we remember, asserting that Inaveguwa did not hold Kuluboku was an important part of Motabasi's defense against a perceived threat. Perhaps Kailimila is telling Motabasi that that threat is not one he need worry about.

77. *La keda, mauula adoki balivala makadana wala.* (That was) His road, therefore I think I will speak that road as well.
78. *Gala Motolala, gala Woiyaii, gala Taubagoni, gala Inaveguwa.* (It is) Not Motolala, not Woiyaii, not Taubagoni, not Inaveguwa.

Motolala	Woiyaii	Taubagoni	Inaveguwa
F [A + U(Kb)]	F [A + U(Kb)]	F [A + U(Kb)]	F [A + U(Kb)] 78

In statement 79 Kailimila gives a reason for Ilawokuva telling him, instead of Motabasi, about the garden. Motabasi at that time was still living in Tukwaukwa, and according to his own account (SS31-34) he did not establish a gardening relationship with Ilawokuva until he moved to Teyava.

79. *Matona igau Tukwaukwa, oluvi bikalobusi Teyava, igau Tukwaukwa.* He (Motabasi) was still in Tukwaukwa, later he would show up in Teyava, (but this was when he was) still in Tukwaukwa.

Kailimila's opening statements (SS77-82) set up the conditions for an important social event. Kailimila presents the event itself as a part of a conversation between himself and Ilawokuva. Ilawokuva's instructions to Kailimila are reported as follows:

80. *Yegu mesiniku wala igau tokubukwabuya yegu.* I was still a young bachelor myself.
81. *Tokubukwabuya yegu, gala kubukwabuya nagowa.* I was a bachelor, but not a bachelor without responsibility.
82. *Bogwa lamilitomwota labugubagula kala biga.* I was already gardening and becoming a man, so to speak.
83. *Labugubagula, mesinaku ikaibiga,* I was gardening, she (Ilawokuva) simply said,
84. *"Kululuwai makwena dakali."* "You remember that (garden at) our fence (Kuluboku)."
85. *"Bogwa imesa vedaiya, bogwa ikausa, mesinaku wala kululuwai."* "Our kinsmen have come and taken it away, but you remember it."
86. *"Bikaliga Solobuwa, kula kukwau."* "When Solobuwa dies, you go get it."

Again, we see the common Trobriand narrative technique of rendering entire conversations as if in direct quotation. The statements reported here gain in meaning by being posited as the utterances of particular actors in particular contexts. In this case, statement 85, in context, is the basis for the instantiation of an entire schema. The proposition that Ilawokuva was *tolibaleko* of Kuluboku can be taken as given by the previous presentations. The kinsmen who came, Solobuwa and his group, are of the same major clan as the litigants but are of a different *dala* and thus are not owners. In order to come and get the garden they would have had to come with *pokala,* and would have had to have been allocated use rights to the garden by Ilawokuva.

Statement 86 is very interesting because, embedded as it is in the context of an instruction from Ilawokuva to Kailimila, it has two aspects, each of which instantiates a schema. On the one hand, Ilawokuva projects the event of Kailimila recovering Kuluboku from Solobuwa into the future. On the other hand, instructing Kailimila to recover the garden gives him the right to do so.[1] That is, this statement appears as both of the following propositions:

```
   Kailimila    A(Kb)   Ilawokuva
[          ] ◄——— [            ] 86 illocutionary force
```

```
   Kailimila       katuyumali      Solobuwa
[ A(Kb) ] ————————————————► [ U(Kb) ] 86 locutionary force
```

Each of these propositions calls an entire schema, so that this whole structure can be modeled as shown in Table 9. The interpretation here relies much more on prior knowledge than the interpretation of any of Motabasi's statements. This is not surprising since the utterance is reported as a statement made by Ilawokuva to Kailimila in a particular context. Given that situation, the statement is completely unambiguous.

It is clear that Kailimila is going to pursue a different course of argument than that employed by Motabasi. In this episode, Kailimila shows use rights to the garden being allocated out of the owning *dala,* an event which Motabasi did not mention at all.

We see that the schemata not only provide a structure for making interpretations of actual and hypothetical events, but they can be used in the formulation of plans of action as well. They are the knowledge structures which specify the organization of culturally meaningful event sequences. If plans are cognitive representations of meaningful event sequences which include certain events and states and exclude others, then schemata are certainly involved in the conception of plans. Ilawokuva's statements constitute a plan for the recovery of Kuluboku by Kailimila as a representative of the owning *dala.*

Notice that Kailimila has quoted Ilawokuva and allowed his audience to infer what his own understandings of the events must have been, given Ilawokuva's instructions.

Table 9 Kailimila's first three episodes of discourse

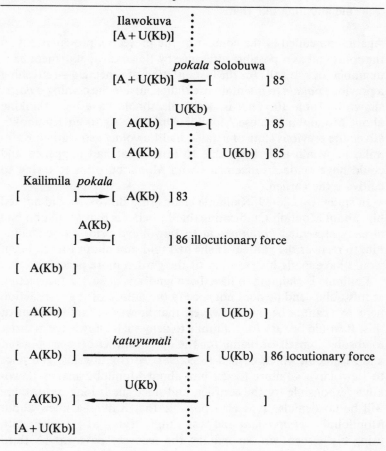

EPISODE 4

In statement 87, however, Kailimila introduces a hypothetical instruction which he claims Ilawokuva did not give to him but which he feels, based on his subsequently acquired knowledge, would have made things much easier for him.

87. *E, sitana bilukwegu, kawala,* Well, she might have told me something like,
88. *"Kunanamsa sitana pikekita pela matona tokekita isisu, Monilobu."* "You think a bit about the younger man there, Monilobu."
89. *E, bilukwegu, bala sitana bakimanum.* She might have told me and I could have done it in a more peaceful way.

90. *Mitaga gala wala sitana ilukwegu makala.* But she did not tell
me anything like that.

Again, embedded in the context of the preceding presentations to
the court and as a possible utterance by Ilawokuva, statement 88 is
unambiguous. It calls for the instantiation of schema 4—refreshing
a previous *pokala* to maintain use rights outside the owning *dala,* as
shown in Table 10. That is, Kailimila should have been thinking
about Monilobu because Monilobu had use rights in Kuluboku.
Given the previous state of affairs, had Ilawokuva so warned Kailimila, he would have been able to infer what had happened and
could have made arrangements with Monilobu prior to trying to
cultivate the garden.

In statements 86–89, Kailimila claims that Ilawokuva did not tell
him about Monilobu, indicating that he believes that Monilobu had
already presented *katumamata* to Ilawokuva prior to her telling
him to recover the garden. If she had told him about Monilobu, it
would have made his recovery of the garden more peaceful.

Kailimila is claiming to have been ignorant of such a transaction
at this point, and he does not specify the nature of the transaction
here. We cannot be sure, however, that he was in fact ignorant of
this. It would be easy for Kailimila to deny such knowledge in order
to absolve himself of blame for the open conflict between himself
and Monilobu which ensued (SS92-98). Attributing his ignorance
to Ilawokuva's failure to tell him about Monilobu makes Ilawokuva responsible for the conflict, and since she is long dead, there
will be no denials. It is also possible that Kailimila knew about
Monilobu's *katumamata* and was simply trying to get away with
using his garden without making the recovery payment. A third

Table 10   Kailimila's fourth episode of discourse

	Teyava village "owners"		Oyveyova village "nonowners"	
Ilawokuva			Solobuwa	
[A(Kb)]			[U(Kb)]	
		katumamata		Monilobu
[A(Kb)] ◄———————————————————			[	]
				U(Kb)
[A(Kb)]			[	]◄—[ ]
[A(Kb)]				[U(Kb)]

possibility is that Monilobu had not yet *katumamata'*ed at the time of Ilawokuva's instruction to Kailimila. Ilawokuva may have told Kailimila to get the garden, and later, when Monilobu brought *katumamata,* Ilawokuva either forgot or neglected to tell Kailimila about her subsequent decision. In any case, we again see the importance of having up-to-date information. Kailimila's actual state of knowledge at that point is not essential to the outcome of the case between himself and Motabasi. The proceedings of the court case between Kailimila and Monilobu will temporarily resolve the confused relations of men to this garden. As rhetorical dressing, it is important for Kailimila to appear to enter the conflict as a victim of someone else's failure of social responsibility rather than as an aware instigator.

EPISODE 5

Kailimila reports the proceedings of the case between himself and Monilobu as follows.

99. *Itowesa kala biga policiman, kaunsera, ibwabusa.* The police and counselor stood back, so to speak, and cut the case (announced their decision).
100. *Ikaibigasi,* They said,
101. *"Gala bukuvagisa yowaii."* "Don't make it a fight."
102. *"Kululuwai, Kailimila, besa vavagi bogwa ela Oyveyova."* "Kailimila, you remember, this thing has already gone to Oyveyova."
103. *"Ela Oyveyova, bogwa iyosisa tomumwaiya."* "It has gone to Oyveyova, the old men (Solobuwa and Monilobu) already hold it."
104. *"Besa tuta bogwa lewokuva lokuvinokisa korti, bogwa ikau tomwaiya."* "Now you(pl.) have finished the court proceedings, the old man (Monilobu) holds it."
105. *"Besa tuta kululuwai bukula o m valu."* "Now, you remember and go to your village."
106. *"Avaka bukulokaiya, bukwaimali m vavagi."* "Go get whatever you can to recover your thing (the garden)."

Statement 106 is an instruction by the court to Kailimila to assemble a *katuyumali* (return) payment. The appropriate schema is shown in Table 11. Here, we see that the owning *dala* cannot simply do what they please but must respect the rights of others even with regard to their own lands. I am unsure whether Kailimila had to wait for a natural exchange opportunity (for example, the death of someone in Monilobu's *dala*) or if the court mandated an exchange

Table 11   Kailimila's fifth episode of discourse

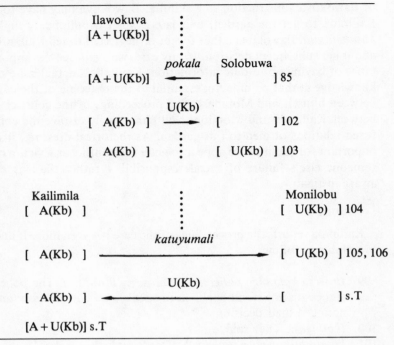

opportunity in order to clear up the issue immediately. In either case, the actual transaction is described in statements 107-109.

EPISODE 6

107. *E, lasobusi tamvasi kuvi, kaiyu tubwaiyagi, kuwayu kikiya, kawatala seniseni.* So, I laid down four ceremonial yams, two arms of bananas, two bunches of betel nut, and a small clay pot.

108. *Besa layaki tomwaiya Monilobu.* This I took to the old man, Monilobu.

109. *"E, bitowa m vavagi."* (He said,) "Your thing goes to you."

Statement 109 presents the actual event of Monilobu giving up his rights in Kuluboku in response to the *katuyumali* presented by Kailimila. It is modeled in Table 12.

This concludes Kailimila's account of how he came to have rights to Kuluboku. He now turns his attention to Motabasi's claims. His first line of attack is to demonstrate the difference between his actual record of involvement with Kuluboku and Motabasi's record. In statements 110-127 Kailimila elaborates on the difference. In

Table 12 Kailimila's sixth episode of discourse

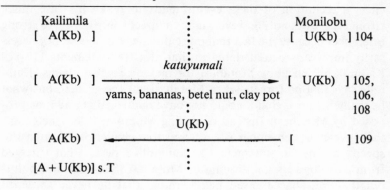

statement 112 Kailimila claims that he was already gardening Kulu-boku when Motabasi moved to Teyava, implying that he would have known if Motabasi had subsequently gardened it.

112. *Pela bogwa lavitau makaina kaivatam, kala biga.* Because I had already begun this *kaivatam,* so to speak.
113. *E galaga bogwa ewokaiyagu,* He didn't go to me (and say),
114. *"Adoki batai kwevyeka ulo baleku."* "I think I will cut a big garden for myself (that is, use Kuluboku)."
115. *Sitana balilagi.* I would have heard if he had.
116. *Gala iwanani makwena baleku.* He never prepared that garden.
117. *Lewa, kaina makateki lewa ikugwa kovitaki, kaina ikugwa kovitaki oluviyekiga lema, lewa Teyava.* He went, perhaps he recently went and took the garden first, or perhaps he took the garden first and then came, he went to Teyava.
118. *Gala anukwali, bogwa lalumwalai, kala biga.* I don't know, I have forgotten, as they say.
119. *Sitana bikatuviyali.* He can explain.
120. *Gala ikalatala, bogwa ilukwem, gala ikalatala.* He didn't (garden it) one day, he told you, not one day.
121. *Yegu, atitaitala, atitaiyu, atitaitolugu.* Myself, I cut it once, I cut it twice, I cut it thrice.
122. *Tolukuyabi ikamda kaiyasa, Tolukuyabi kwevyeka kaiyasa bogwa kunukwalisa sola Togewasi yegu titaitolugu.* Toluku-yabi made a *kaiyasa,* Tolukuyabi had a big *kaiyasa,* as you know, with Togewasi, then I cut it the third time.
123. *Titaivasila Kwemwai, Mekuvi ivagisa wala leliya.* The fourth time Kwemwai and Mekuvi did a bit, but mostly it lay fallow.
124. *Kalavigimkoyluva etomwa.* It stands there at the end.

Since there are witnesses to many of the events which Kailimila cites, a recitation of these events tends to make his case much stronger. It does not, however, make a direct contribution to strong inferences because the fact that one cultivates a plot does not necessarily imply any actual rights to that plot. In statements 117-119 Kailimila is ridiculing Motabasi for making foolish claims. Kailimila says that he forgets when Motabasi got the garden, but what he really means is that it could not have happened at any time proposed by Motabasi. Instead of calling Motabasi a liar, he claims that he cannot remember when it was and challenges Motabasi to specify a time. In statement 120 Kailimila repeats what emerged from Tovalugwa's questioning of Motabasi (SS64-72) and points out that Motabasi himself has admitted that he never gardened Kuluboku. In contrast, Kailimila gives his own gardening record with Kuluboku in statements 121-123. The *kaiyasa* he mentions in statement 122 is a special gardening competition which involves an entire community. People who participated in the *kaiyasa* will likely remember that Kailimila gardened Kuluboku, especially if his harvest was plentiful. At this point, several men in the audience assent to Kailimila's claim saying "Yes. That's true."

EPISODE 7

125. *E, lagela baviguli pela ulo vavagi bogwa lanukwali.* And today I will garden it because I know what is mine.
126. *Malasi wala isakaigu isakaibogegu.* The Malasi people gave it to me first.
127. *Lewa mesinaku wala ibugubagula kala Inaveguwa.* He went and gardened for Inaveguwa.
128. *E, ivagiga mokwita bogwa ilukwemi, ilukwedasi.* Yes, he did as he has told you, as he told us.
129. *Kaiyu kaivatamwa levagi pela minana numwaiya.* He did a bit of *kaivatam* for the old woman.
130. *Ikasali la baleku bogwa kulagisa, Wawawa, Kapwalelamauna, e Bwesakau.* She allocated his gardens as you have heard, Wawawa, Kapwalelamauna, and Bwesakau.
131. *Makwesina kwetolu la baleku.* Those three are his gardens.
132. *Itatai tutala.* He cuts them (regularly).
133. *Gala avaka? Baveva balitaki?* Is that nothing? Should I rise up and cut them?
134. *Avaka pela?* What for?
135. *"Isakaigu vivila, 'Kuma kulitaki.' "* (As if to himself,) The woman gave them to me, (saying) "Come and cut them."
136. *Gala! Gala lakabukwani.* No! I have not touched them.
137. *La vavagi.* They are his things.

138. *Bogwa iseki Malasi la vavagi.* The Malasi people gave him his things.

In these statements, Kailimila twice instantiates the schema for transfer of rights inside the "owning" *dala* (Table 13). The importance of this episode to Kailimila's presentation is that Kuluboku is not among the gardens allocated to Motabasi by Ilawokuva. Woven into this is an appeal for moral parity. Statement 133 is a rhetorical question. Statements 134-135 represent a mock conversation in which Kailimila pretends to justify to himself why he should cut a garden which is not his. He imagines that someone told him to do it. This is a parody of the hypothetical conditions under which Kailimila feels Motabasi may have convinced himself that Kuluboku was his garden to cut. Statement 136 answers the rhetorical question posed in 133. Kailimila insists that since he does not capriciously attempt to garden those plots that are rightfully held by Motabasi, so Motabasi ought not to try to garden plots that are rightfully held by Kailimila.

Near the end of his presentation, Kailimila again refers to the event that most strongly supports his case. (Statements 146-147 refer to the episode shown in Table 14.)

146. *Ala akaimali o yamala Monilobu.* I went and brought it back from the hand of Monilobu.
147. *Bogwa alivala makala.* I have already said this.
148. *Besa tuta biyogagi makeda wala pela ilebu o yamagu.* Now he (Motabasi) would spoil our way by snatching it from my hand.
149. *Kidamwaga bititavila.* As if he would turn things around.
150. *Mesinaku.* That's all.

Table 13 Kailimila's seventh episode of discourse

Ilawokuva				
[A + U(Wa, Kap, Bwe)]				
		pokala	Motabasi	
[A + U(Wa, Kap, Bwe)]	◄———		[ ] 129	
	kaivatam			
	A + U(Wa, Kap, Bwe)			
[ ]	————————►		[ ] 130, 138	
	[A + U(Wa, Kap, Bwe)] 131, 137			

Table 14 Kailimila's eighth episode of discourse

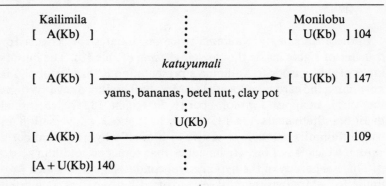

SUMMARY OF KAILIMILA'S PRESENTATION

Kailimila has given an account which moves in a credible fashion to the proposition

Kailimila

[A + U(Kb)]

It does so without confronting Motabasi's defenses against such a claim.

Kailimila grants that Motabasi's assertions are true for the three gardens Wawawa, Kapwalelamauna, and Bwesakau, but not for Kuluboku. According to Kailimila, Kuluboku has quite a different history. Use rights in Kuluboku go out of the owning *dala* to Solobuwa in response to *pokala*. Rights of allocation—the responsibility to recover the use rights—go to Kailimila. The use rights are later transferred to Monilobu in an event which is left unspecified by Kailimila. It is not important that Kailimila specify the event in which the use rights are transferred to Monilobu, because the result of the transfer is restated in the outcome of the court case which followed between Kailimila and Monilobu. The decision of a court hearing performed in public is a more tangible event than an exchange which may have taken place with only a few witnesses present. As reported by Kailimila, part of the court decision was an instruction to him to recover his garden through *katuyumali*. Kailimila's report of that recovery concludes his account of his own relation to the garden. Kailimila's account is rendered more credible by his reference to public events such as the court case and the *kaiyasa* in which he gardened Kuluboku.

It is interesting that Motabasi's presentation supplies information which can bring resolution to a vague area in Kailimila's presentation. In episode 4 of Kailimila's presentation, the existence of a *katumamata* (renewal) payment from Monilobu to Ilawokuva can be plausibly inferred but is not described by Kailimila. Now, Motabasi describes an exchange event in which Monilobu presents one arm of bananas to Ilawokuva. Motabasi, on the assumption that Ilawokuva had not yet allocated any rights in the garden, mapped this event onto the concept *pokala,* and concluded that one arm of bananas was insufficient. Given Kailimila's assertion that use rights in Kuluboku had already been allocated to Solobuwa (Monilobu's older brother), this very same exchange event maps onto the concept *katumamata.* Thus, Motabasi's attempt to defend against an anticipated argument unwittingly provides evidence which supports Kailimila's actual argument.

Motabasi's confusion over the conceptual identification of the exchange event he witnessed is no doubt exacerbated by the layered polysemy of the term *pokala.* As was noted in Chapter 3, *katumamata* is a marked term in a contrast set in which *pokala* is unmarked. Figure 9 shows the terms as nodes in a tree.

When, according to Motabasi's quote, Ilawokuva said, "Come eat this arm of bananas, the old man's *pokala*" (S43), Motabasi took it to be the specific *pokala*(2), while it appears Ilawokuva intended the general level *pokala*(1) which subsumes *katumamata*(3). Likewise, when Motabasi quotes his brothers as saying that they have already *pokala*'ed for the garden (S25), he again takes them to mean specifically *pokala*(2). Kailimila's presentation makes it clear, however, that they meant *pokala*(1) which subsumes *katuyumali*(4). This confusion left Motabasi trying to instantiate the wrong relation (that is, *pokala* instead of *katumamata* in one case, and *pokala* instead of *katuyumali* in the other). It is no wonder he was able to refute the most likely instantiations of these irrelevant relations.

As of the end of Kailimila's presentation, the double interpretation of Monilobu's giving of bananas to Ilawokuva has not been overtly stated. In the course of the testimony of witnesses and the discussion which follows, this problem is stated with increasing clarity.

The Testimony of Witnesses

Following Kailimila's presentation, Motabasi's younger sister, Inaweya, testifies that the garden was never allocated to anyone in Oyveyova village. She claims that Ilawokuva gave Kuluboku to Motabasi.

After some discussion, more witnesses arrived. It was decided that instead of allowing the litigants to reconstruct their presentations to the court, the bailiff Tovalugwa should summarize the ar-

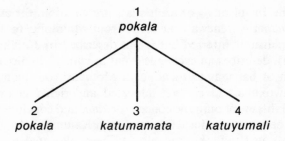

Figure 9. *Marked and unmarked* pokala *types*

guments for the witnesses. The testimony of the various witnesses is lengthy. In that testimony, the following major points arise: The headman of Motabasi's and Kailimila's *dala* comes to the support of Kailimila by saying that Solobuwa did hold the garden, but criticizes both litigants for having brought this intra-*dala* dispute into the public domain. Upon hearing his headman's testimony, Motabasi says he did not know the garden had already been allocated. He insists that if it had been, Ilawokuva would have told him. This is a risky thing for Motabasi to say because this sort of statement can work against as well as for Motabasi's case. Motabasi is sure that Ilawokuva did not tell him about having allocated the garden, but he has no direct evidence that she did not allocate it. The absence of an event is of course more difficult to establish by observation than the presence of the same event. Motabasi must therefore support the assertion that she did not allocate the garden by inference. If it is assumed that Ilawokuva informs Motabasi of all of her dealings, then from the observation that she did not tell him, it can be plausibly inferred that she did not allocate it.

But under what conditions would such an assumption be justified? It is justified only if Motabasi is Ilawokuva's only heir. If it can be independently demonstrated that Ilawokuva did allocate the garden to Solobuwa, and yet did not tell Motabasi about it, then Motabasi is shown to be less close to Ilawokuva than he would have the court believe. Thus, asserting that Ilawokuva did not tell him can be used to defeat the proposition that she allocated it only if it is assumed that Ilawokuva wanted Motabasi to know about the garden. On the other hand, the same assertion can be used to defeat the proposition that Ilawokuva wanted Motabasi to know about the garden if it is shown that she did give the garden to Solobuwa.

In response to Motabasi's claims, the headman of Motabasi's *dala* simply repeats his statements to the effect that Ilawokuva did give the garden to Solobuwa. Here, Motabasi's own statements begin to discredit his case. Sibwekewa, a respected village elder, states the problem most clearly, "You see, Monilobu gave no *pokala*. They say Solobuwa. Solobuwa *pokala*'ed, not Monilobu. Monilobu simply gave *katumamata* to Ilawokuva."

The histories of the garden Kuluboku (Kb) as presented by the two litigants are summarized in Tables 15 and 16. A comparison of these histories shows clearly that the point of divergence between the presentations occurs at the interpretation of the nature of Monilobu's presentation of bananas to Ilawokuva.

Kwaiwai's Opinion

Following more discussion of court procedure, Tovalugwa invites members of the court to state their opinions. The members of the court are the village leaders who, while the local government council was operational,[2] were appointed to hear the cases. Members of the court include the *guyau* (chief), the elected local government council committee members, and hamlet headmen. According to court protocol, witnesses should provide evidence only, not opinions. Members may give opinions and suggest judgments.

Kwaiwai is heir apparent to the present *guyau* and was formerly a local government council committee member. Unlike the aging *guyau*, Kwaiwai is young (late 20s), dynamic, assertive, and charismatic. He is obviously an intelligent man who offers consistently lucid explanations. In the center of the village, where crowing roosters, barking dogs, screaming children, and gusts of wind all vie for a place on the ethnographer's tape recording, I greatly appreciated Kwaiwai's powerful voice and unhurried delivery.

KWAIWAI:

151. Motabasi supported the old woman.
152. That's fine, nothing wrong there.
153. Kailimila, that's fine, nothing wrong there.
154. However, this garden . . .
155. Within (the argument) if it had been *tupwa*, you all understand.
156. You all know how it is with *kaivatam* and *tupwa*.
157. But this garden was not *tupwa*.
158. It was already allocated.
159. For this reason, I think, my hearing of the case was that this garden was already allocated.
160. If it had been *tupwa*, no one would worry, Motabasi, it would be your garden.
161. Because of being *tupwa*, it would be your garden.
162. But because it had already been allocated,
163. So, it went to Oyveyova.

Table 15 Summary of Motabasi's history of the garden

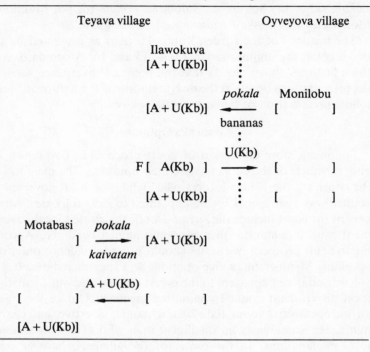

164. Oyveyova, I heard you say that you stood and saw Moni-lobu's one arm of bananas.
165. Yes, but it was allocated.
166. This is called warming up the *pokala* of his companion.
167. And the old woman gave it to his companion.
168. So it came here, and therefore it runs on.
169. My hearing, my bystander's opinion is:
170. If it had been *tupwa,* no one would worry, Kailimila would not take it today.
171. It would be your thing.
172. But because it had already been allocated,
173. It went to another village.
174. It went there.
175. And it returned here.
176. Therefore, I think its clarity emerges.
177. If it had been *tupwa,* it would be your thing.
178. Kailimila would sit down.
179. Because of your *kaivatam* and it being *tupwa.*
180. And whatever within it was not in the likeness of allocation, Kailimila would sit down.

Table 16 Summary of Kailimila's history of the garden

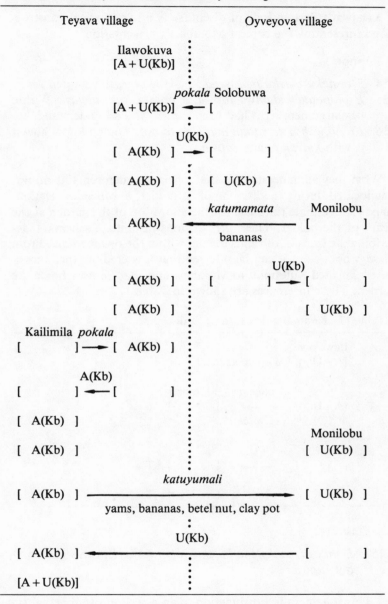

181. But because it had already been allocated, fine I say, let it be allocated.
182. This is my thought having listened critically to what the two of you have said.
183. My thought is finished here.

Analysis of Kwaiwai's Opinion

Kwaiwai's first episode of discourse is a hypothetical construction representing the core of Motabasi's presentation.

EPISODE 1

154. *Mesinaku baleku makwena* . . . However, this garden . . .
155. *E olopoula kidamwa tupwa, e bogwa kukwatetasi.* Within (the argument) if it had been *tupwa,* you all understand.
156. *Kunukwalisa kaivatam makaina tupwa.* You all know how it is with *kaivatam* and *tupwa.*

What they all understand is that when a garden remains *tupwa,* unallocated during the lifetime of its holder, a *kaivatam* relationship is a legitimate rationale for the allocation of the garden at the death of the holder. These propositions instantiate schema 1 describing the transfer of rights to land within the owning *dala.* From these propositions it can be inferred that it is credible that Ilawokuva allocated Kuluboku to Motabasi and that he now holds the garden. These inferences are shown in Table 17.

Table 17   Kwaiwai's first episode of discourse

Ilawokuva
$[A + U(g)]$ 155 —hypothetical

$$[A + U(g)] \quad \overset{pokala}{\underset{kaivatam}{\longleftarrow}} \quad \text{Motabasi} \quad [\qquad] \ 156$$

$$[\qquad] \quad \overset{A + U(g)}{\longrightarrow} \quad [\qquad] \ \text{p.T}$$

$$[A + U(g)] \ \text{p.T}$$

EPISODE 2

157. *E mitaga, makwena baleku gala tupwa.* But this garden was not *tupwa.*

This statement is a disjunction to an assertion of an actual state which conflicts with the entry conditions for the previous unit. Applying the truth value "false" to the lead proposition of episode 1 yields the reassignment of truth values for the same set of propositions as shown in Table 18. From this assertion it can be strongly inferred that Ilawokuva did not allocate the garden to Motabasi in response to his *pokala,* and from that it can be plausibly inferred that Motabasi never came to hold Kuluboku.

Table 18   Kwaiwai's second episode of discourse

Ilawokuva
F [A + U(g)] 157

$$[A + U(g)] \xleftarrow[\text{\textit{kaivatam}}]{\textit{pokala}} \quad \text{Motabasi} \quad [\qquad] \, 156$$

$$[\qquad] \xrightarrow{A + U(g)} \quad [\qquad] \, s.F$$

$$[A + U(g)] \, p.F$$

EPISODE 3

In statements 158–159 Kwaiwai sets up the specification of the model which will compete with the hypothetical interpretation given in episode 1. These statements (which are mapped in Table 19) are also further repetitions of the foundation of the reassignment of truth values of episode 2.

158. *Bogwa kasesila.* It was already allocated.
159. *E besa uula ananamsa ulo ligalega wala makwena baleku bogwa kasesila.* For this reason, I think, my hearing of the case was that this garden was already allocated.

Table 19   Kwaiwai's third episode of discourse

Ilawokuva
[A + U(g)]

$$[\quad ? \quad] \xrightarrow{R(g)} \quad [\qquad] \, 158$$

EPISODE 4

Statements 160 and 161 are a simple reiteration of episode 1 (Table 20).

160. *Kidamwaga tupwa, gala avela bininaiyuwa, Motabasi, mitaga
     m baleku.* If it had been *tupwa,* no one would worry, Mota-
     basi, it would be your garden.
161. *Pela tupwa, e, besa m baleku.* Because of being *tupwa,* it
     would be your garden.

Notice here that the connective "because," or *pela* in Kiriwinian,
stands not only for several logical relations but also for the unstated
propositions which are required to make the connection between
the two stated propositions.

Table 20   Kwaiwai's fourth episode of discourse

Ilawokuva
$[A + U(g)]$ 160—hypothetical

<pre>
                    pokala   Motabasi
    [A + U(g)]   ◄———   [   ] 156
                    kaivatam

                    A + U(g)
    [   ]   ———►   [   ] p.T

                    [A + U(g)] p.T 160, 161
</pre>

EPISODE 5

In statements 162 and 163, Kwaiwai begins to specify the content
of the model only hinted at in episode 3.

162. *E, mitaga pela kasesila bogwa ivilobogwa,* But because it had
     already been allocated,
163. *E, ela besa Oyveyova.* So, it went to Oyveyova.

Given the context of the previous presentations, these statements
unambiguously instantiate the relations shown in Table 21. These
relations invoke schema 2 describing the transfer of use rights out
of the owning *dala.* From this it can be surely inferred that Solobuwa provided some sort of *pokala* to Ilawokuva even though that
event is not overtly mentioned. Thus, Kwaiwai's fifth episode
forms the core of the argument which will compete with the hypothetical argument proposed in his first episode.

Table 21   Kwaiwai's fifth episode of discourse

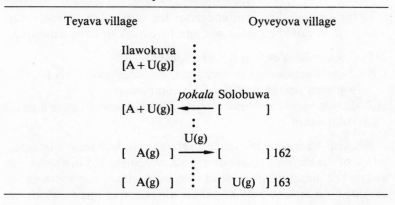

Teyava village   Oyveyova village

Ilawokuva
[A + U(g)]

                    pokala Solobuwa
[A + U(g)] ◄——— [   ]

                    U(g)
[A(g)] ———► [   ] 162

[A(g)]   [U(g)] 163

EPISODE 6

164. *Oyveyova, alagi m bigatona kukwaibiga kutota besa tomwai-ya Monilobu e usi wala kaitala.* Oyveyova, I heard you say that you stood and saw Monilobu's one arm of bananas.

This statement refers to episode 4 of Motabasi's presentation in which Motabasi asserts that the one arm of bananas is insufficient as *pokala* for the garden. That assertion being true would make it credible that Ilawokuva did not allocate use rights in Kuluboku to Monilobu. The inference is shown in Table 22. The final state of this episode is required for entry into the core episode of Motabasi's presentation which appears here hypothetically in episode 1.

Table 22   Kwaiwai's sixth episode of discourse

Ilawokuva
[A + U(g)]

                    pokala   Monilobu
[A + U(g)]   ◄———   [   ] 164
                    bananas

                    U(g)
[A(g)]   ———►   [   ] s.F

[A(g)]   [U(g)] p.F

EPISODE 7

In this episode Kwaiwai addresses the crux of Motabasi's mis-interpretation of the exchange event he claims to have witnessed.

165. *E kasesila.* Yes, but it was allocated.
166. *Yagala makwena titavana wala, e besaga sola.* This is called warming up the *pokala* of his companion.
167. *E numwaiya iseki besa sola.* And the old woman gave it to his companion.

Whereas statement 164 made a reference to Motabasi's interpretation of the exchange event as *pokala,* statement 165 in disjunction asserts the inappropriateness of that proposition and replaces the episode built around it by Motabasi with another one in which the event—Monilobu giving bananas to Ilawokuva—is modeled on the *katumamata* schema in Table 23. Given that reinterpretation, the next assertion (S167), that Ilawokuva allocated use rights to Monilobu, is made credible.

Table 23 Kwaiwai's seventh episode of discourse

Ilawokuva	:	Solobuwa		
[A(g)]	:	[U(g)] 165		
katumamata or *titavana*			Monilobu	
[A(g)] ◀——————————			[ ] 166	
bananas				
	:		U(g)	
[A(g)]	:	[ ] ——▶	[ ] p.T 167	
[A(g)]	:		[U(g)] p.T	

EPISODE 8

168. *E besa lema, mapela isaitaula wala.* So it came here, and therefore it runs on.

Statement 168 differs from previous statements in an important way. The referent is the garden, conceived of as moving conceptually across a social space. This statement says something about the *keda,* or path, of the garden (see Chapter 3). It is a statement which describes a higher level of discourse organization than any previous statement. The reader will recall that as a formal structure, the model of semantic information representation has a property called recursion. That is, a proposition relates a group of concepts to each other, and a proposition is also itself a concept. A relation among propositions is therefore also a proposition. We have, of course, encountered propositions on these levels in the discourse considered so far. A statement such as "He gave *pokala* to her" is a simple proposition. A statement such as "She gave him the garden because he gave *pokala* to her" is a more complex structure relating two propositions to each other. Applying the recursion once more, we generate a proposition which asserts a relation among units, each of which asserts a relation among propositions. Each episode in discourse, being modeled on a schema for a transfer of rights, asserts a relation among a set of propositions. The structure generated here, then, asserts a relation among units of discourse. Each unit describes a step in the social movement of the garden. An assertion about the relations of the steps is a description of the *keda,* or path, of the garden.

Statement 168 demonstrates the heuristic power of a process of recursive embedding of progressively more complex units. The metaphor of the movement of gardens in this case allows for the concise representation and expression of relations among relations among relations among concepts.

EPISODE 9

Statement 170, addressed to Motabasi, again returns to the hypothetical construction given in episode 1.

170. *Kidamwa tupwa, gala avela bininaiyuwa, gala lagela Kailimila bikau.* If it had been *tupwa,* no one would worry, Kailimila would not take it today.
171. *M vavagi.* It would be your thing.

As before, the hypothetical construction shown in Table 24 is stated only to be countered by a disjunction to an assertion of an event which precludes the truth of the hypothetical proposition.

Table 24 Kwaiwai's ninth episode of discourse

Ilawokuva
[A + U(g)] 170 —hypothetical

	pokala	Motabasi	
[A + U(g)]	◄────	[ ] 156	
	kaivatam		

	A + U(g)		
[ ]	──►	[ ] p.T	

p.T [A + U(g)] 171   Kailimila
p.F [A + U(Kb)] 170

EPISODE 10

Statements 172-174 are a reiteration of episode 5.

172. *E mitaga pela kasesila bogwa ivilobusi,* But because it had already been allocated,
173. *isunapula ela o valu kwetala.* it went to another village.
174. *Lela.* It went there.

Like statement 164, these statements refer to the truth of an entire episode of discourse (shown in Table 25) rather than to a single proposition within an episode. It is a reaffirmation of the truth of the structure generated in episode 5 which described Solobuwa's acquisition of use rights.

Table 25 Kwaiwai's tenth episode of discourse

Ilawokuva   ⋮ Oyveyova village
[A + U(g)]   ⋮
                 ⋮
                 ⋮
                pokala Solobuwa
[A + U(g)] ◄──── [   ]
                 ⋮
          U(g)   ⋮
[A(g)   ] ──► [   ] 172
                 ⋮
[A(g)   ] ⋮ [U(g)   ] 173, 174

EPISODE 11

175. *Ikaiita lema.* And it returned here.

As with the statement above, this one refers to whole episodes of discourse. In this case it refers to episode 5 of Kailimila's presentation in which he describes his recovery of the garden from the hand of Monilobu. Given the context of the statement, there is no need for Kwaiwai to elaborate on the details of the return of the garden. That episode in Kailimila's presentation is the only one in the corpus of the case which describes the return of a garden. That schema is shown in Table 26.

Statement 176 is like 168, up a level. It is a qualitative description of the overall organization of the relations among units of discourse.

176. *Mapela adoki kala migileu bisunapula.* Therefore, I think its clarity emerges.

The metaphors used in the description of the organization of discourse are revealing. They often evoke qualities of linearity of progression (for example, *saitauli,* runs straight without diversion; *duosisiya,* straight; *nigwanigwa,* tangled; *itasikula,* it snags on/ movement is arrested by something; *vitububwati,* lines up with/is coterminous with) or of clarity of vision (*migileu,* clear; *kala gigisa bwena,* fine in appearance). The act of rendering a decision in a case, thereby ending all arguments, is referred to through the metaphors *tatai,* to cut; *bwabu,* to lop off; and *kapituni,* to decapitate. Here, Kwaiwai's statement 176 integrates episodes 9, 10, and 11. The "clarity" of the case "emerges" from these episodes. They describe the portion of the history of the garden in which the presentations of the litigants become incompatible.

Table 26   Kwaiwai's eleventh episode of discourse

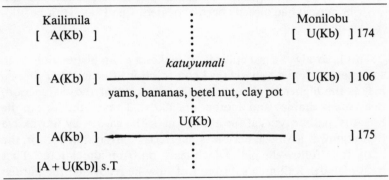

EPISODE 12

In statements 177-180 Kwaiwai returns for one last time to the hypothetical construction which began his presentation.

177. *Kidamwaga tupwa, m vavagi.* If it had been *tupwa,* it would be your thing.
178. *Kailimila bisisu.* Kailimila would sit down.
179. *Pela kaivatam, tupwa.* Because of your *kaivatam* and it being *tupwa.*
180. *E avakaga olopoula makala kasesila gala, o Kailimila bisisu.* And whatever within it was not in the likeness of allocation, Kailimila would sit down.

These propositions can be expressed in the notation as shown in Table 27.

Table 27 Kwaiwai's twelfth episode of discourse

Ilawokuva
[A + U(g)] 177 —hypothetical

	pokala	Motabasi	
[A + U(g)]	◄———	[ ] 179	
	kaivatam		

	A + U(g)		
[ ]	———►	[ ] p.T	
		Kailimila	
p.T [A + U(g)] 178		F [A + U(Kb)] 178	

EPISODE 13

181. *Mitaga pela bogwa ilokasesila, bwena aluki bilokasesila.* But because it had already been allocated, fine I say, let it be allocated.

This is Kwaiwai's last episode. It makes a clean disjunction from statement 177, the hypothetical construction. Beyond that, it also makes the higher level assertion that because of the disjunction, one *keda* is enabled and another precluded. That is, the fork in the litigants' paths occurs at the allocation of the garden by Ilawokuva to Solobuwa. Kwaiwai here says in effect, "Given that fork in the path, fine, follow the path which leads on from allocation." That path includes Kailimila's account of how he recovered the garden from Monilobu but precludes Motabasi's account of how Ilawokuva gave him the garden in response to his *kaivatam*.

The Chief's Decision

Following Kwaiwai's opinion, the chief conferred for a moment with the members of the Local Government Council. On many cases they actually instruct him in what to say. In all cases I observed, the chief himself announced the decision, giving it the weight of his authority.

Murebodema's decision was as follows:

MUREBODEMA:

184. *E, adoki Motabasi gala bukugibuluwa.* Perhaps you will not be angry, Motabasi.
185. *Kidamwaga tupwa, bogwa ilivala Kwaiwai, kala tupwa besa, m vavagi.* If it was *tupwa*, as Kwaiwai said, the *tupwa* would be your thing.

186. *E, besaga pela bogwa ikasilabogwa* . . . And here, because she (Ilawokuva) had already allocated it . . .

MOTABASI (now screaming):

187. *Gala! Bogwa bamapu Monilobu la pokala biwa.* No! I will match (Kailimila's) *pokala* to Monilobu.

188. *Gala kudoki avela biyosi manakwa baleku.* Don't assume anyone else will hold that garden.

189. *Lagela wala bamapu, gala nabweya.* Today, I will pay the *pokala,* not tomorrow.

MUREBODEMA:

190. *E, bakapitila wala.* I will make the decision.

191. *E, avaka ninami inanamsa, baleku Kailimila biyosi.* Regardless of what you think, Kailimila will hold the garden. (In the background, Motabasi claims he will kill a pig as part of the *pokala.*)

192. *Igau, avaka m nanamsa kulosa deli veyamwa, mi karewaga.* Later, whatever you (Motabasi) can think of with your kinsmen, that is your(pl.) business.

193. *Kai! besa wala: adoki Kailimila biyosi.* Hey, just this: I suppose Kailimila will hold it.

MOTABASI:

194. *Pela gala anukwali la pokala tomwaiya.* Because I didn't know about the old man's (Solobuwa's) *pokala.*

TOVALUGWA:

195. *Bogwa kulagi!* Well now you have heard!

MOTABASI:

196. *Igau, bitakalawasi la pokala Monilobu.* Wait! Let us(inc. pl.) recount the *pokala* to Monilobu.

197. *Bamapu wala lagela biwa.* I will reimburse him (Kailimila) today.

TOVALUGWA:

198. *Gala bukuvagisa makala!* Don't you do this!

MOTABASI:

199. *Gala, bamapu wala, pela manakwena tayakali.* No, I will pay it today for it is why we dispute.

TOVALUGWA:

200. *Besa bukuvagisa, igau bigaga senela.* If you do this, things will be very bad later.
201. *Ambesa kam vilavila Motabasi* . . . Whatever is your share, Motabasi (refers to the three gardens he did receive from Ila-wokuva) . . .

MOTABASI (speaking over Tovalugwa's statements):

202. *Pela gala teyuwela.* Because there is no other.
203. *Ilukwegu luguta gala teyuwela.* My sister told me there is no one else.

TOVALUGWA:

204. . . . *Oluvi, ambesa Kailimila biyosi la vavagi.* After that, whatever else is Kailimila's he shall hold.
205. *Motabasi, gala kukwaiyatetila bukukwabukwani.* Motabasi, you shall not reach out for, you shall not touch.

From here on, the case disintegrates into a shouting match. Kaili-mila claims that if Motabasi tries to reimburse him for the *pokala* he gave to Monilobu, he will give even more to Monilobu's heirs, making it harder for Motabasi to catch up. Motabasi, incensed, rejects that notion, screaming, "As if it is Oyveyova's land?" Tova-lugwa forcefully tells them to be quiet and reannounces Murebo-dema's decision. Motabasi stomps dramatically off toward his hamlet, yelling fiercely, "I want to repay their *pokala.* I will live to take that land!" A man with experience as a government clerk in-jects some borrowed Western wisdom, saying that the one who yells the loudest is the thief, the quiet one is the true rights holder.

As the proceedings break up and people begin to leave to go to their gardens, Tovalugwa threatens that if the decision of the court is not observed, they will call Waibadi, the second highest ranking chief on the island, to come and hear the case.

Annotation of Murebodema's Decision

Murebodema makes no new inferences on his own, but cites Kwaiwai's opinion (especially episodes 1 and 5) and gives a decision which makes Kwaiwai's opinion the opinion of the court.

Motabasi's proposal to reimburse Kailimila for the *pokala* Kaili-mila gave to Monilobu, and Kailimila's counterproposal to give even more *pokala* to Monilobu's heirs, are both unprecedented constructs which are outside the representational scope of the schemata of land tenure. The court will not accept Motabasi's proposal, and Tovalugwa warns Motabasi to leave those thoughts.

He says that things will be bad later if Motabasi attempts such an exchange. I believe the way things will be bad is that such events cannot be modeled with the existing knowledge base. The history of rights in the garden will be difficult to trace in future years. Such breaches of procedure may allow the garden to become "lost" to its owners.

CONSEQUENCES OF THE DECISION

As a result of the decision, Kailimila is allowed to use the garden Kuluboku. Motabasi has suffered a loss in prestige. He has been shown to have been lacking knowledge of lands he claimed to control. In the least charitable interpretation of his attempt to cut the garden and subsequent defense in court, his behavior can be seen as intentionally deceitful. In the most charitable interpretation, he is at best *iudawadi,* mouthing it, talking through his hat, or claiming knowledge which he does not have. Knowledge is power in such situations, and the demonstration of his lack of knowledge is a blow to his prestige. The decision is all the more embarrassing for Motabasi because on the basis of his incomplete knowledge he committed one of his followers, Modalewa, to cutting the garden. The initial cutting of the garden is hard work, and Modalewa has simply wasted whatever time he put into it. Modalewa would be quite justified in being angry at Motabasi.

5 | Uses of the Cultural Code

TERMS SUCH AS problem solving, planning, understanding, decision making, and explanation are often taken as descriptors of cognitive processes. In light of the uses of the cultural code observed in the previous chapter, I take them not to be descriptors of various distinct processes so much as descriptors of the conditions under which, or the task environments in response to which, the cultural code (as a process) is applied. Many different types of processes could perform each of these tasks under different conditions. Conversely, some instances of each of them can be performed by the processes of instantiation and inference on the cultural code, as the following discussion will show. In many cases the system of use of the cultural code has properties of its own which go beyond the formal properties of the model itself; these emergent properties and the way they arise from the implementation of the cultural code will be described. Although the cultural code modeled here is not sufficient to account for all of the relevant phenomena, this model and the analysis of it demonstrates the potential for larger models of a similar nature to account for a substantial portion of the organization of meaning in discourse.

Abbreviate Discourse, Reconstruct Abbreviated Discourse

The most obvious observation on the analysis of this case is that the connectedness of discourse depends to a large extent upon propositions which do not appear as statements in the text. As a string of symbols, every presentation to the court was profoundly incomplete. A procedure which recovers untransmitted information by filling in, where necessary, propositions or whole groups of propositions is required to preserve semantic continuity. In the analysis above, I have shown that the schemata of land tenure as described in Chapter 3 provide a representational structure on which such a procedure can be defined.

The procedure has at least two major subroutines. They are: (1) identifying an event in the environment (or a description of an event) as an instance of a particular concept in the conceptual system, and (2) using that identification to derive information about other concepts in the system.

A description of the way we identify events in the environment as instances of a particular concept has of course been a central goal in psychology and cognitive anthropology for some time, and I will not attempt a review of the vast literature on this subject. I would simply like to contribute a few observations made on an analysis of on-going natural discourse.

Many models of the process of instantiation are represented in terms of exclusively bottom-up or stimulus-driven processes. The distinctive feature models, taxonomic analysis (numerical or otherwise), componential analysis, prototype analysis, and additive feature models all rely on a fundamentally bottom-up routine. Neisser (1976) and others have at times argued for a top-down, goal-oriented, constructionist representation of this process. I am not qualified to speak for what happens at the level of perception, but I will try to show here that as we move toward more abstract and complicated conceptual structures, both the cognitive schemata and the features of the events themselves contribute to the construction of the representation.

Consider the class of exchange behaviors which were defined in Chapter 3 (*pokala, katumamata, katuyumali,* and so on). When a Trobriander is thinking about land tenure, identifying an event as an instance of an exchange concept means embedding a representation of that event in one of the transfer schemata. At several points in this case a single event has been interpreted as being an instance of different concepts when embedded in different schemata. Since there are many schemata, the assignment of an event as an instance of a concept must involve the choice of a schema on which to model the events observed. This choice is in part stimulus driven. For each unit of discourse the questions which had to be answered were: (1) where (in social space) is the garden relative to the owning *dala,* and (2) where might it be moving relative to the owning *dala.* Figure 10 is a flow diagram which shows which differences make a difference in choosing a schema as a model for events.

As inputs to the process of choosing a schema on which to model an event, the essential properties of the event itself are (1) the *dala* membership of the participants, and (2) the direction of exchange.

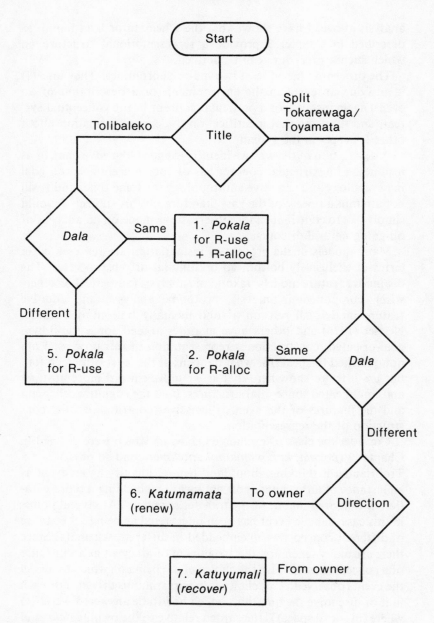

Figure 10.　*Flow diagram for choice of schema*

To the extent that the choice of a schema depends upon these inputs, the process of interpretation is stimulus driven. But the meaning of the event also depends upon the prior distribution of titles in land (the entry conditions of the schema), which are elements of the meanings of previous events. As noted earlier in Chapter 2, titles cannot be directly observed but only inferred from the observation of other events through the use of the schemata: Thus, two sets of inputs, one from the environment and one from an organized semantic memory, are required for the choice of a schema onto which the event can be mapped as an instance of a particular constituent concept. Without changing the properties of the event which are attended to, a change in the believed prior distribution of titles can change the meaning of the event by causing it to be mapped onto a different schema.

This is what we observed in Motabasi's interpretation of Monilobu's presentation of bananas to Ilawokuva. Motabasi interpreted that event on schema 2 as an instance of *pokala* between *dala*. Kwaiwai and the court, operating on information which established a different distribution of titles in the garden prior to the event, interpreted it on schema 4 as an instance of *katumamata*—the waking up of previous *pokala* between *dala*. In this case, the prior distribution of titles to the land established the *context* of the event. That is, it supplies that portion of the information which is required for mapping the event onto the conceptual system but which is not contained in the properties of the event itself. To the extent that the process relies on the properties of the event, it is a bottom-up process. But to the extent that it relies on previously organized structures in semantic memory, it is a top-down process.

Having once mapped an event onto a schema, the processor can use the structure in top-down processes in several ways. First, an incompletely instantiated schema can be used to guide the search for missing concepts. Motabasi's attempts, in episodes 5, 6, and 7 of his presentation, to counter anticipated claims by Kailimila are clearly the product of such a search guided by the incompletely instantiated schema in his first episode of discourse. Another top-down use for the structure is in the use of inference processes to assign truth values to propositions which represent events and states which have not been, or cannot be, observed. In the analysis presented here I have attempted to show how pervasive such inferences are.

Every major schema represents some degree of redundancy in the system. Given a schema and a proposition within it, it is possible to infer the truth values of other propositions within the episode. Those inferred propositions are therefore redundant in the sense that they contribute no new information to a receiver of a message, provided that the receiver understands the proposition and knows which schema to instantiate. Because of this feature it is possible for a speaker who shares the code with his listeners to omit from his verbal accounts statements which embody propositions, the truth values of which can be inferred from others included in the discourse. The listener will be able to reconstruct the abbreviated discourse by applying the underlying schema and the inference routines. This function has been modeled by Schank and Abelson (1977) in computer simulations of script-based understanding. They call it "script application" because it involves the application of a knowledge structure they call a script to a story which represents experience. Knowing which schema to instantiate is clearly a major problem for the understander.

Experimental evidence on memory errors and false recognition indicate that these filling-in processes are automatic (Bower, Black, and Turner, 1979). The system always tries to complete an episode by fully instantiating a schema and applying inference procedures to derive truth values for all propositions in the episode. It is assumed that the system generates and stores those propositions which are not observed but which are required to complete the episodic account, even when truth values cannot be assigned to them.

This abbreviation and reconstruction is, of course, only effective where speaker and listener share the code on the basis of which the abbreviation is made. Where this is not the case, the abbreviated discourse appears at best cryptic and at worst unintelligible to the listener. The conversational postulate (Grice, 1975) that one should not say more than is needed to convey the meaning intended is based in the ability of the hearer to use a knowledge structure such as the schema to fill in the discourse, and in the speaker's belief that the necessary knowledge structure is available to the hearer.

Since all of the propositions about titles to land and many of the propositions about exchange events must be inferred, most of what is "known" in this domain is not known directly. It is inferred. The majority of the propositions that make up an individual's experience of social reality are not read directly off that reality but are instead inferred on the basis of a cultural conceptual consensus about what combinations of states and events can and cannot be true. If anything, the analysis presented here gives an impoverished impression of the extent to which an individual's knowledge of his world is a product of inference. It models only the barest skeleton of the conceptual knowledge that a Trobriander brings to the interpretation of discourse in this domain.

Stimulus-driven models give a good account of many-to-one mappings of events onto concepts, that is, where many events can be instances of any given concept. In categorization tasks this is the usual nature of the problem. When we consider the process of categorization of instances as it occurs in natural reasoning activities, however, the observed mapping is many-to-many. Several distinct events may all be instances of the same concept, yet any single event may satisfy more than one concept in the representational structure. The importance of realizing that the semantic structure is a network rather than a tree is that it forces the realization that in order to resolve ambiguities in the classification of certain instances, top-down constraints as well as bottom-up feature analysis will have to be involved.

Our experience of reality is not what is in our world; it is what we think is in our world. What we think is out there is shaped by what we expect to be out there and what we believe cannot possibly be out there. Some readers may find the idea that most of our understanding of our world is a case of computation by active construction (albeit a shared construction) to be somewhat counterintuitive. We normally assume that we see and understand the world as it really is. We do not usually think of the sense that we make of the world as being the product of computations at all. Subjectively it just happens. We observe some aspect of the world, and either we know what is going on, or we do not. But we are unlikely to consider the nature of the processes that generated our understanding. Considering the job that our understanding facilities have to do for us, it would be quite disturbing for us to be continually aware of how much of our representation of our current reality is derived from inference.

Chunking

The fact that the initial and terminal components of the basic structural units (schemata) are state descriptions allows the units to be concatenated to form larger and more complex meaningful units. An episode begins and ends with a proposition which specifies a particular person's rights in a particular garden. A sequence of such episodes describes the *keda* or path of the garden among persons and social groups. The use of the *keda* metaphor is an even more powerful abbreviation device than that described in the previous section. With it, an entire episode can be represented in discourse as a single statement. When Kwaiwai says the garden went to Oyveyova and came back (SS173-175) he has described a series of events in the world which when fully spelled out occupy sixteen propositions. Black and Bower (1979) have shown that memory for specific events within episodes in discourse depends upon the number of events within the episode, but not on the number of other episodes in the discourse. The *keda* metaphor allows the speaker to refer to the individual episodes in the discourse in terms of the most salient events within them. Of course, the amount of knowledge the listener needs in order to expand such radical abbreviations is considerable. Here, more than simply the underlying schema and the inference routines must be shared. In order for such a chunk to be meaningfully understood, the understander must also share with the speaker a number of propositions which represent specific historical events. Partial understanding is, however, possible in the absence of the historical details. Even lacking knowledge of the details of the case, the implications of Kwaiwai's statements may be inferred by anyone familiar with the cultural code.

Understanding and Explanation

There is no simple criterion for judging when understanding has or has not taken place. Some understandings are more profound than others, but in every case understanding involves the embedding of observations of events in a network of unseen causal connection. An event is "understood" when it is represented as a component of a larger episode, or concurrently as a component of several episodes at once.

To minimally explain an event, one must communicate a representation of that event as a component of an episode. As noted above in the sections on abbreviation and chunking, however, the communication of an entire episode does not always require the overt symbolic representation of all the components of an episode. When the listener already has the appropriate schema, explanation can be brief. It may consist of nothing more than a clue to get the listener to the right schema. This was the case when Sibwekewa explained that it was Solobuwa who gave *pokala* while Monilobu only gave *katumamata*. This utterance explained the event by explicitly stating which type of event the prestation of bananas was. The schema defines the minimum context in which the event can be understood or explained. Where context is not fully specified, the listener will have to provide context by choosing a schema on which to model the propositions. As we saw with Motabasi's misunderstanding of Monilobu's *katumamata* prestation of bananas, the way the event is understood depends on the schema in which it is modeled and on the truth values assigned to the propositions within the episode.

When the listener lacks the appropriate schema, as ethnographers and children so often do, the explanation may be structured to impart the organization of the schema as well as the content of the thing being explained. In the absence of a metalanguage for the description of schemata, giving prototypic exemplars is an effective mode of communication. This is why so many of the explanations elicited by the ethnographer come in the form of conditional statements describing what sorts of things happen in various circumstances.

The essential property of the episode as a model of some aspect of the world is that it makes assertions about a domain of discourse. The "difference which makes a difference" in the world is made apparent in the representation it is given by the application of the code, but the code itself is referentially transparent to its users. It is the vehicle for assertions about the world, but it is not, and probably should not be, the vehicle for assertions about itself. Like the grammar of a language, the cultural code is invisible to those who use it. It is invisible because it is not a set of propositions about the world but a set of instructions for the construction of propositions.

I am not asserting that culture does not contain any propositions about how the world is. Such propositions—the prototypic cultural beliefs—are very likely an important part of culture as it was defined in the introduction. I am asserting, however, that a more complete understanding of culture in general, or cultural belief systems in specific, can be achieved through the explicit representation of the cultural code that organizes the propositions which are taken by anthropologists to be beliefs, norms, or values. Consider the case of language again. Every user of a natural language probably has a set of already formed sentences stored for use. Conventional greetings, lines from songs, plays, or poems, are all parts of a language user's repertoire, but they are not the grammar of the language. Such stored sentences may have a role in speech production in certain circumstances, but they are totally inadequate as a description of how language is understood or how new sentences are formed. The code, having been built on the analogy to the grammar of a language, is capable of generating a large number of propositions, yet it is not the propositions that it generates.

Problem Solving

The use of the explanatory function of the cultural code is exploited in litigation to perform a complex sort of problem solving. Each litigant must produce a culturally meaningful account of the history of a garden which terminates in the state in which the litigant himself has rights in the garden. The problem is well solved if the litigant can also show that there exists no culturally meaningful history of the garden which terminates in the state in which the opponent has rights to the garden in question. In some respects the problem solving task of the litigant is akin to theorem proving in mathematics or logic. The cultural code provides the axioms or implicit premises of the system. The historical background of the case, and especially the state in the past at which the litigants agree on the disposition of the garden, provides the explicit premises of the problem. The theorem to be proved is a proposition which represents the litigant's own rights in the land. The proof consists of a demonstration that a path exists. The solution requires that the litigant assemble evidence—in the form of instantiations of the component relations of the schemata—which gives the strongest possible demonstration of the existence of a garden transfer path that ends in his hands. The strength of the path depends upon the strength of the inferences which are required to provide truth values for those propositions that cannot be verified by the testimony of witnesses. If many of those inferences are plausible inferences, as was the case with Motabasi's presentation, then the account may be plausible and culturally meaningful but not compelling. Kailimila's case was more compelling because it ultimately rested on the public proclamation in a previous court decision to the effect that he should give *katuyumali* to Monilobu and recover his garden.

Judgments of Sense, Truth, and Likelihood

Motabasi's presentation was a sensible account until Kailimila spoke. Kailimila's presentation made Motabasi's presentation nonsensical, or impossible as an explanation. How did this happen? Motabasi's presentation depended upon a particular proposition being true at a particular point in time. That proposition, that Ilawokuva had both use rights and rights of allocation to Kuluboku, was, along with the proposition that Motabasi gave *pokala* to her, a necessary condition for her allocation of the garden to him. Kailimila's presentation demonstrated that Motabasi's own account excluded the possibility of that proposition being true. The truth of that proposition was excluded from possibility not by observation but by inference performed on the representation. Ilawokuva's prior decision to allocate use rights in the garden to Solobuwa entailed the negation of the proposition on which Motabasi relied. In statement 157 Kwaiwai asserts that the enabling condition is false, and in statement 162 he gives the reason for it being so. Because of the strength of the inference, there is no need to explicitly state that Ilawokuva did not allocate the garden to Motabasi. (In fact, to do so would only antagonize Motabasi.)

That the truth values of these propositions are established by inference rather than by observation should not be surprising, since it was noted in Chapter 3 that one of the properties of man's relation to his world of experience is that when discrete existentially quantified propositions are in question, a single observation is sufficient to establish that a thing has happened but no practical number of observations is sufficient to establish that it has not. In the schemata of land transfers, those propositions which represent specific events can be assigned the truth value "true" by observation or by inference, but they can be assigned the truth value "false" only by inference. Those propositions which represent states (rights in land) can be assigned truth values either "true" or "false" only by inference. The relations between men and land are abstractions which are not directly observable. The analysis I performed on other domains of discourse in the Trobriand Islands make it clear that many of the semantic relations involved in the interpretation of experience, especially social experience, in any society are relations which refer to events and states which are not directly observable. More of our knowledge of the world than we probably realize is arrived at through inference.

Assessments of likelihood are the products of plausible inferences. The plausible inference routines are heuristically valuable to the processing system because they provide information about the relative likelihoods of propositions in circumstances where strong inferences are not supported. Propositions representing either states or events can only be assigned truth values "more likely" or "less likely" by inference. In the analysis of the discourse we saw how frequently plausible inferences were required to maintain the continuity of discourse. Because of the fluidity of the linkage between logical connectives and underlying logical relations (see Chapter 3) plausible inferences are not always marked as such in discourse. Statements of likelihood often masquerade as statements of fact.

Decision Making

The decision of the court on the disposition of the garden presents yet another use of the cultural code. In models of decision making which are based on utility theory, a decision is made by assigning utilities to the possible outcomes and choosing the outcome which maximizes some utility. In litigation, the decision constitutes a choice of a social outcome, and the possible outcomes of the case could be assigned social utilities. The decision, however, does not appear to be based on the social utilities of the outcomes. An examination of Kwaiwai's opinion (which became the official opinion of the court) shows that the criterion of decision revolves around the cultural meaningfulness—the interpreted possibility or impossibility of the presentations.

Expectations and Plans

Since it is in the formal character of the logical relations to constrain the possible combinations of truth values of linked propositions, the schemata can be used in certain conditions to establish expectations and to formulate plans. Both plans and expectations are symbolic representations of future states of events in which some states or events are included and others are excluded. Kailimila gives a report of a plan which was communicated to him as part of his presentation to the court. Ilawokuva instructed him to recover the garden Kuluboku upon the death of Solobuwa (S86). That is, in the presence of a particular condition (the death of Solobuwa), the performance of a particular act, *katuyumali*, will accomplish a goal (the recovery of the garden Kuluboku by the owning *dala*). The organization of the plan, a set of temporally sequenced conjectured propositions, is provided by the schemata. They provide just the sort of knowledge one needs to influence the course of events. Assessments of the likelihood of success of a plan can be arrived at by the application of the inference procedures to the representation.

Expectations regarding what will happen or is likely to happen can clearly be generated through the application of the cultural code. Given a particular current state, some episodes may meaningfully be expected to follow while others will be precluded. Expectations are interesting because the violation of expectations contains new information about the world. When everything conforms to expectations, the processing system can simply match expectations to observations, and nothing in particular need be noticed. When expectations are violated, further processing may be required to discover how to integrate the violating observations into a meaningful representation. Several sorts of conditions can lead to the violation of expectations. First, one may have based expectations on a faulty prior assumption. This happened to Motabasi, of course, with regard to the status of the garden Kuluboku. Second, one may attempt to model the relevant events on an inappropriate schema. This also happened to Motabasi because of his having gotten the facts wrong. Third, the knowledge base may simply fail as a model of experience. This could happen in social situations because other actors do not organize their own behavior in accordance with the accepted cultural code. Where this is the case their behavior will be judged deviant. The knowledge base could also fail because it is simply not appropriate to the observations at hand. This happens often in cases of cross-cultural misunderstandings, where the knowledge structures of the alien are incapable of producing meaningful interpretations of the events witnessed. It is also the case when observations outreach the range of theory in science.

Violations of Expectations

The properties which give the cultural code its referential transparency also give it near empirical closure. In our normal modes of interpretation of experience, the burden is upon the world to make sense. When there is a failure of fit, we usually suspect that something is wrong with the world. We rarely imagine that something is wrong with the procedures we use to make sense of the world. We can often make sense out of things we didn't expect, but we seldom expect not to be able to make sense of experience. Since the cultural code is a set of instructions about how to construct assertions in a domain of discourse, rather than a set of such assertions, no single simple proposition can violate the cultural code. In order to violate the cultural code, two or more simple propositions must arise such that no available cultural schema can accommodate them. If one or more of them violates the expectations established by the interpretation of the other(s) on all appropriate schemata, then the propositions are in logical contradiction. A violation of expectations is a proposition which cannot be accommodated by the schema on which the observed event was being modeled. Violations of expectations are often resolved by reinterpreting the experience in terms of another schema.

Suppose an individual is unable to find a suitable interpretation for some part of his experience. What does the system do in such a case? Just as the grammar of a language does not change in response to every ungrammatical sentence which is produced, neither does the cultural code change for some small number of violations. The violations of the code are interpreted or understood as events or episodes which are nonsensical or not understandable or not meaningful. They are not interpreted as being false, because to be either true or false, a proposition must be meaningful. Motabasi's presentation to the court was labeled false by the court, but it was credible; it was meaningful.

Attribution

The apparent stability of experience no doubt derives in part from the short-run near empirical closure of the interpretive apparatus. There are, however, other sources. Given the model presented here, we might want to account for some of that stability with a dynamic model in which it is assumed that those who share culture will be planning their own acts and interpreting the acts of others with the same cultural code. While we don't really know the extent to which this is true, the belief that it is so is probably important to the actors in the system. An important use of the cultural code which depends upon this belief is the attribution of internal states to social actors as a part of the interpretation of their behavior. The attribution models of personality psychology (Heider, 1958) conceive of the process of interpreting the behavior of others as involving the attribution to those others of intentions, motives, desires, feelings, and so on. Heider says that one way to do that is to imagine "what would I do, think, feel, want, if I was in his place?" In Heider's scheme the thought, feeling, intent, and so on arrived at can be attributed to the other as a part of the interpretation of his behavior. But how does one arrive at the internal state to be attributed to the actor? Heider's proposed heuristic of imagining oneself in another's shoes does not directly allow one to attribute an intent or a feeling to the actor; rather, it allows one to attribute to oneself the state of knowledge and the cultural code of the actor. That is, one performs an implicit simulation of the other person's processing. From that simulation, which depends on the assumption of a shared cultural code, the intent, feeling, or expectation of the other can be computed.

In litigation, the presentations of the litigants themselves are not rich in such attributions, because the court protocol requires that they give only reports of facts, not interpretations of the facts. The commentary provided by those who witness litigation, however, is rife with assertions about the wants of the participants in the case. The organization of such attributions clearly depends on the use of the cultural code. What is attributed to the social actor is not simply an internal state but a system of knowledge and a mode of processing. From that attribution, the intent or feeling of the actor is computed. Motabasi reported Ilawokuva saying to him, "Come eat the old man's *pokala*. He thinks it has already gone inside his fence" (SS43-45). The interpretation of that statement by Motabasi himself or by anyone listening to the case requires the following essential assumptions: (1) that Monilobu is constructing his behavior in accordance with the cultural code (planning an event which is enabled by his *pokala*), (2) that Ilawokuva is interpreting Monilobu's behavior with the same code (understanding which event the *pokala* enables her to perform), and (3) that Ilawokuva has attributed that code to Monilobu (to infer what he was planning). This quite complex representation is easily and automatically achieved by all those who use the cultural code of Trobriand land tenure.

The use of the attribution of the cultural code in the interpretation of the behavior of social actors adds to the apparent stability of experience. It does so not by making experience necessarily any more stable but by adding to the flexibility of the interpretive system. When the interpretation of behavior involves the attribution of the cultural code, then the meaning of behavior is no longer simply a function of the properties of the behavior itself but is rather a function of the complex internal processes in the actor which are believed to have contributed to the production of the behavior. This complexity is apparent in our Western folk and formal notions of the evaluation of behavior. Once we know what an actor did, we need also know whether he "meant" to do it (or in our courts, whether he knew the consequences of his act) in order to evaluate his action. The flexibility of interpretation which derives from using the cultural code for attributions gives the system additional interpretive latitude because one can nearly always infer a set of post-hoc internal states that can be imagined to account for the observed actions.

For an act to be interpreted as meaningful, it has to be understood as the product of a process which is based on the cultural code. Social acts are evaluated not by comparison with a list of proper behaviors but by examination of the expected possible consequences of the act, and the actor's alleged awareness of the culturally defined consequences of the act. The attribution process, then, requires at least two cultural schemata. One, like the land-tenure schemata presented in the preceding chapters, provides the template for the formulation of plans. The other schema must encode information about the relation of a person's thinking to his behavior. When someone gives *pokala* to his mother's brother, for example, it is the land-tenure schema which allows a witness to know what states that act may enable. If there is reason to assume that the actor shares the model of land tenure, the witness may attribute it to him. But the attribution of some part of the cultural code to a social actor is based on the unstated premise that there is a relation between the thinking of the social actor and his acts. It is based on an assumption that what the actor does depends upon what he knows and how he thinks about it.

This assumption provides a good example of the referential transparency of such structures. In our culture we take the relation of the actor's knowledge to his action so much for granted that it is difficult to persuade people that it is part of their belief system. I have had informants tell me that it was not part of the belief system, but a feature of the world. It may well be both, but this response is typical of the way users of a cultural code refuse to regard the code as a structure which mediates their experience.

Given this other schema, the act of *pokala* becomes an instance of different concepts in two different episodes which do different sorts of work. Interpreted in the land-tenure schema, the act of *pokala* provides information about other events in an episode in the world of events, namely, that the likelihood of an allocation of land to the person who has given *pokala* is increased. Interpreted in the attribution schema, the act of *pokala* is a social act which provides information about the state of knowledge and intents of the actor: he is operating in accordance with the principles of land tenure, and he intends to get land by giving *pokala*.

The attribution schema is a very general one. It can be applied to any domain for which there exists a set of functional schemata like those presented here for land tenure. In fact, while the application of the attribution schema relies on the existence of a set of functional schemata which are specific to a domain of discourse, statements about the relations between the internal states of actors and their acts often outnumber statements about the relations between the states and events of the experience itself. In a study of "why" questions, Piaget noted that the propositional conjunction "because" "is used most commonly to express diffuse psychological rather than logical or causal relations between events (e.g., 'I'll do thus and so because I want such and such.')" (Flavell, 1963, p. 275). It should be noted, however, that the diffuse psychological relations posited among events are based on logical or causal relations. In the absence of a structure which specifies logical conjunctions among semantic relations in the world, it is impossible to plan, and impossible to attribute plans to others.

Speech Acts

Another task which requires simultaneous multiple instantiations of schemata is the interpretation of speech acts. The analysis of statement 86 in the discourse given in the previous chapter shows how a performative utterance is understood to be both a statement about the world and an act in it. As a statement about the world, the speech act is a symbolic representation of an event in the world. That event is understood by incorporating it in an episode based on a schema about the functional relations of events. The proposition which is so generated can be stored as a thing which was said about the world, that is, as a representation of a representation of the world. As an act in the world, the speech act—as a social behavior itself—is understood in the same way that the statement about the world was, except that the proposition which results from the application of the understanding procedure to the act aspect of the speech act is stored as a representation of something which happened in the world rather than as something that was said about the world.

6 | Conclusion

THE PRECEDING CHAPTERS present one possible model of a cultural code for a very restricted portion of a domain of discourse. The model gives a plausible account of the role of such a structure in the generation and interpretation of experience. It is a model of an aspect of native understanding which (to my knowledge) has not previously been described for naturalistic data in a non-Western society.

This project represents a synthesis of a number of issues in cognitive science and approaches to the study of cognition that has not previously been attempted.

If what we want to know about is how people reason in the real world, let's look at them doing that. The usual assumption is that the real world is too messy to study directly, so artificial situations are created in which observations are made. On the whole, however, I feel that the analyst's task is no more difficult in the field setting than in the laboratory. The impression that this cannot be so rests primarily on unjustified assumptions regarding the extent to which the behavior of subjects in experimental settings is directly revealing of cognitive processes. Whether the setting is experimental or natural, the investigator must be able to make and support assertions about the representation of the task that the subject brings to the task's solution. The laboratory setting has its advantages, but so has a more naturalistic environment in which assertions about the representation are supported by ethnography rather than by the experimenter's hope that the subject understood what is being asked of him. Here I have attempted to tackle the real world head on, and I hope that this work may lead to the development of reliable procedures for the study of cognitive processes in natural settings.

When looking at natural cognition, there can be no illusions about studying either process or representation in isolation from the other. The strategy of inferring the nature of process from the observation of task performance is retained. But now the definition of the task is given by the culture rather than by an experimental design. The way culture defines the nature of the task can only be seen when some relevant part of culture is given explicit representation. I have attempted to solve the problem of giving culture explicit representation by exploiting another convergence of interests. A slight modification of the traditional methods of anthropology and ethnography provide a specification of the content and organization of the task, and the philosophy and tools of the artificial intelligence methodology provide the means for giving the cultural knowledge explicit representation.

Part of the original charter of cognitive anthropology was the dictum that it is more important to discover the appropriate questions than it is to discover the answers to questions. In terms of the schema theoretic approach, the appropriate questions in any situation are questions about propositions which need to be instantiated in order to achieve an unambiguous interpretation of the events at hand. Knowing the appropriate questions is evidence that one knows at least implicitly how the relevant schemata are organized. That knowledge is what the ethnographer needs in order to understand what he observes, but it is not yet sufficient to explain how what is observed is understood. Using the notion that a model should be sufficient to do the task it explains, I have presented a notation in which the cultural knowledge discovered via anthropological techniques is explicitly represented. The model so constructed mimics the inferences made by natives when they interpret discourse and reason about events.

Perhaps the most ambitious aspect of the study involves the fact that the analysis was performed on naturally occurring discourse in a society and language very different from our own. It is here that the reader will be least able to evaluate the adequacy of the analysis. I have made the mappings of the discourse onto the conceptual structure in a way that seems to me true to the language and the culture. But because it would involve a detailed explication of the Trobriand language itself, I have not made the justifications for that mapping explicit throughout. I can only ask that the reader consider the consistency of the account as evidence that the translations from Trobriand language to conceptual structure are appropriate.

The picture of natural reason among the Trobrianders that emerges from this study is one of a highly interactive process, interactive both in the sense of the simultaneous participation of many people, and in the sense that an interpretation of reality is settled into through the interaction of many processes and many sorts of knowledge. The model satisfies some of the original expectations about what a cultural code might consist of and what it might do. Here is a knowledge structure which implicitly discriminates between the possible and the impossible. It is the embodiment of a set of decision procedures which generate assessments of truth and likelihood which are the same as those made by informants. It defines a structural unit which is the episode of discourse.

How many schemata does an adult user of any culture need to have? At the level of specificity of the schemata described here, a great many must be required to capture the knowledge that an ordinary person in any culture has about his or her world. One may well wonder if any person has the memory capacity to accommodate the number of schemata required by their observable abilities. It must be remembered, however, that even though a great many schemata may be required, there is considerable redundancy in related groups of schemata, so that the total information that must be stored to represent a large number of schemata is nowhere near the sum of the information storage requirements of the individual schemata. Still, the job of determining just what a person would need to know in order to lead a normal life in any culture is so overwhelming that we are not likely to know how many schemata are necessary for some time to come.

Through this study I have come to the conclusion that culture is not a list of ideas, nor even a set of propositions. Some part of culture or the cultural code must consist of more general and abstract processes which provide intra- and interpropositional organization. In the attempt to discover and describe these processes, this study has focused on form rather than content. The extent to which the reader is able to make sense of the events reported is one measure of an ethnography, and I do hope that the events of litigation are clear. But that is not the standard by which I would like to see this work judged. The goal has not been to teach the reader how to understand Trobriand litigation but to show how Trobriand litigation is understood.

The analysis of litigation has shown that a model of folk logic developed from purely western sources is quite adequate as an account of the spontaneous reasoning of Trobriand Islanders. It is not straight Aristotelian logic, because it contains plausible as well as strong inferences, but then so does our own reasoning. There is no need to posit a different logic, whether alogical (Levy-Bruhl, 1910, 1923), preoperational (Piaget, 1951), or three-valued "L-3"

(Cooper, 1975). The clear difference between cultures with respect to reasoning is in the representation of the world which is thought about rather than in the processes employed in doing the thinking. It is clear that Trobrianders cut the world into a different set of categories from those we entertain, and that those categories are linked together in unfamiliar structures. But the same types of logical relations underlie the connections of propositions in our conceptions and theirs, and the inferences that are apparent in their reasoning appear to be the same as the inferences we make.

Even given the incompleteness of the model, I believe that giving this small part of the system of Trobriand land tenure an explicit formal representation is valuable because when such models do not work, it becomes apparent immediately. The writing of this book took place as a dialectic in which the ethnography and the formal model evolved together. Some of the points in the ethnography (the three types of rights in land in particular) were discovered because the formalism, when constructed without them, failed to model the discourse. Malinowski (1965) left the model of land tenure implicit and blurred the differences between types of rights by using the gloss "ownership" to refer to all three. Powell (1956) and Weiner (1976) each distinguished two types of rights but collapsed the right of allocation and the ownership relation into one category. In retrospect it is easy to see how they did so. Since the right of allocation implies that one is an owner, the only case where it is possible to have one without the other is where a person is an owner without the right of allocation. That case is one of those propositions which occurs frequently but which no one (not even the participants to the system) notices much, because an owner without the right of allocation has no control over the land. The necessity of making this discrimination explicit became apparent only when an attempt was made to analyze the discourse with a model that did not incorporate this distinction. This is, I think, a nice example of the sort of ethnographic knowledge which is easily acquired implicitly by the ethnographer but which is unlikely to enter our awareness unless we are careful to represent that knowledge explicitly. By setting the goal of describing a model that is sufficient to perform the task, the anthropologist can bring some formal rigor to otherwise impressionistic field methods.

To use culture to understand, and to understand culture, are two quite different things. We all do the former, but to do the latter we must study the properties of the cultural code itself. This book is an attempt to make culture the object rather than the instrument of analysis.

Notes
References
Glossary
Index

Notes

1 Introduction

1. This effect is seen in the rigidity of distinctive feature analysis, and is especially apparent in the organization of cognitive models which are derived from quantitative data through the high technology techniques of factor analysis, hierarchical clustering, and multidimensional scaling.

2. D'Andrade (1976) notes several problems that result from giving distinctive features this dual role.

3. See Conklin's (1972) bibliography of folk classification which contains nearly 5,000 entries.

4. D'Andrade et al. (1972, p. 52) offer some speculations on the relation between organizational properties of specific domains and the adequacy of various representational devices.

5. Both Mexican and American subjects were tested. The Americans responded on a five-point scale which was later dichotomized.

2 Trobriand Land Tenure

1. See Frake (1964) for a discussion of performance-oriented ethnography.

2. See Document VII, The Garden Lands of Omarakana (Malinowski, 1965, vol. 1, pp. 430-434).

3. For a full description of Trobriand myths of origin and ownership see Malinowski (1965, vol. 1, chaps. 11 and 12; 1954, pp. 111-116), Powell (1956, pp. 401-408), and Weiner (1976, pp. 164-166).

4. In some contexts Malinowski glossed *toli* with the English "master" and in others with the Melanesian pidgin "Bilong en." The real meaning of this word is wider than that of "master," conveying a sense of responsibility as well as authority, but certainly narrower than that of "bilong en" since it is not applied to trivial material possessions.

5. The singular possessive forms when applied to land usually indicate the presence of other individually exercisable rights in addition to the *tolipwaipwaiya* relation.

6. The unity of the descent group is most apparent in the *sagali* mortuary exchanges.

7. Cf. Malinowski (1965, vol. 1, p. 346).

8. This is not a fixed rule in any sense. While the core of a hamlet may be made up of mature men of one *dala,* men of other *dala* with their nuclear families often also reside. Most often these others are the sons of the members of the core *dala.*

9. This fact, which is demonstrated by Malinowski's own data (Document VII in Malinowski, 1965, vol. 1, pp. 430-434), makes nonsense of his assertion (pp. 198 and 353) that the males of a *dala* grow yams for their sisters on *dala* lands so that the women of the *dala* eat of the produce of the *dala* lands which they do not inhabit. For a particular man gardening for a kinswoman, it will be true in some years that he gardens his sister's yams in his own *dala* lands, but in other years his village may garden a *kwabila* that belongs entirely to a different *dala.*

10. Virtually all males begin their gardening career with a garden of this sort (cf. Weiner, 1976, chap. 6).

11. The holder of use rights later reciprocates by making a presentation of valuables, *takola,* to the person who provided *kaikeda.* As with all Trobriand exchange, the important aspect is the construction and maintenance of an enduring relationship rather than a set of one-time matches of item for item.

12. Cf. Powell (1956, p. 410) for a comparison of *pokala* and *urigubu* as prestations to persons of higher rank.

13. Cf. Malinowski (1965, vol. 1, pp. 190-196) for *urigubu* as tribute to chiefs.

14. Malinowski (1922) describes offerings to spirits inhabiting important geological features as insurance against disaster on *kula* voyages.

15. See Weiner (1976) for a description of some other segments in this wider domain of exchange.

16. Weiner (1976) discusses the ways in which women provide for the regeneration of more than the physical existence of the *dala.*

17. That is, newlyweds reside primarily in the village of the groom's father rather than in the village of the groom's mother's brother.

18. Cf. Powell (1956, p. 390).

19. In the Trobriand language the syntactic markers indicating plural number in nouns do not attach to the nouns themselves.

20. Weiner (1976, p. 159) presents an example of such a case.

21. Cf. Weiner (1976, p. 151).

22. Cf. Malinowski (1965, vol. 1, pp. 188f) for a complete discussion of the sociology of *urigubu.*

3 The Model

1. For the sake of economy this relation, which in a true function notation would occur as $A(g) + U(g)$, will be written $A + U(g)$.

2. Scripts are a type of knowledge structure developed by the Yale artificial intelligence program. They are fully described in Schank and Abelson (1977).

4 Case Analysis

1. In this respect, such a reported utterance has some features of the class of utterances called "speech acts." While a performative utterance accomplishes the act it describes by simply describing it (for example, I thank you), this utterance accomplishes a necessary precondition for the act it describes.

2. Early in 1973 a young man named John Kasaipwalova was elected head of the Kiriwina Local Government Council. In the absence of many council members, he managed to get the members to vote to dissolve the council. Since that time, the Trobriand Islands have been without formal representation to the National Government of Papua New Guinea.

References

ABELSON, R., AND J. CARROLL. 1965. Computer simulation of individual belief systems. *American Behavioral Scientist* 8:24-30.

ATKINS, J., AND L. CURTIS. 1969. Games, rules, and the rules of culture. In *Game theory in the behavioral sciences,* ed. Ira Buchler and H. G. Nutini. Pittsburgh: University of Pittsburgh Press.

BEATTIE, J. 1966. *Other cultures.* London: Routledge and Kegan Paul.

BLACK, J. B., AND G. H. BOWER. 1979. Episodes as chunks in narrative memory. *Journal of Verbal Learning and Verbal Behavior* 18:309-318.

BOWER, G. H., J. B. BLACK, AND T. J. TURNER. 1979. Scripts in comprehension and memory. *Cognitive Psychology* 11:177-220.

BURLING, R. 1964. Cognition and componential analysis: God's truth or hocus-pocus. *American Anthropologist* 66:20-28.

CASAGRANDE, J. B., AND K. L. HALE. 1967. Semantic relationships in Papago folk definitions. In *Language in culture and society,* ed. D. Hymes. New York: Harper and Row.

CHARNIAK, E. 1972. Towards a model of children's story comprehension. Ph.D. diss., M.I.T. AI TR-266.

COLBY, K. M. 1964. Experimental treatment of neurotic computer programs. *Archives of General Psychiatry* 10:220-227.

———. 1967. Computer simulation of change in personal belief systems. *Behavioral Science* 12(3):248-253.

COLE, M., J. GAY, J. GLICK, AND D. SHARP. 1971. *The cultural context of learning and thinking.* New York: Basic Books.

COLE, M., AND S. SCRIBNER. 1974. *Culture and thought: a psychological introduction.* New York: John Wiley and Sons.

COLLINS, A., AND M. R. QUILLIAN. 1972. How to make a language user. In *Organization of memory,* ed. E. Tulving and W. Donaldson. New York: Academic Press.

CONKLIN, H. A. 1972. *Folk classification: a topically arranged bibliography.* New Haven: Yale University, Department of Anthropology.

COOPER, D. E. 1975. Alternative logic in 'primitive' thought. *Man* 10:238-256.

D'ANDRADE, R. G. 1976. A propositional analysis of U.S. American beliefs about illness. In *Meaning in anthropology,* ed. K. H. Basso and H. A. Selby. Albuquerque: University of New Mexico Press.

D'ANDRADE, R. G., N. QUINN, S. NERLOVE, AND A. K. ROMNEY. 1972. Categories of disease in American English and Mexican Spanish. In *Multidimensional scaling: theory and application in the behavioral sciences,* vol. 2: *Applications.* New York: Seminar Press.

FILLENBAUM, S. 1977. Mind your p's and q's: the role of content and context in some uses of *and, or,* and *if.* In *The psychology of learning and motivation,* ed. G. Bower. New York: Academic Press.

FLAVEL, J. 1963. *The developmental psychology of Jean Piaget.* New York: D. van Nostrand Co.

FRAKE, C. O. 1961. The diagnosis of disease among the Subanum of Mindanao. *American Anthropologist* 63:113-132.

———. 1964. Notes on queries in ethnography. In *Transcultural studies in cognition,* ed. A. K. Romney and R. G. D'Andrade. *American Anthropologist Special Issue* 66(3):132-145.

GOODENOUGH, W. 1957. Cultural anthropology and linguistics. In *Report of the seventh annual round table meeting on linguistics and language study,* ed. P. Garvin. Georgetown University Monograph Series on Languages and Linguistics, 9.

GRICE, H. P. 1975. Logic and conversation. In *Syntax and semantics, 3: Speaker acts,* ed. P. Cole and J. Morgan. New York: Academic Press.

HEIDER, F. 1958. *The psychology of interpersonal relations.* New York: John Wiley and Sons.

HENLE, M. 1962. On the relation between logic and thinking. *Psychological Review* 69:366-378.

KAY, P. 1966. Ethnography and theory of culture. *Bucknell Review* 19(2): 106-113. Originally read at American Anthropological Association Annual Meeting, Detroit, Michigan, December 1964.

LEE, D. D. 1940. A primitive system of values. *Philosophy of Science* 7(3): 355-379.

———. 1949. Being and value in a primitive culture. *Journal of Philosophy* 48:401-415.

LEVY-BRUHL, L. 1910. *How natives think.* (French) Translated 1966. New York: Washington Square Press.

———. 1923. *Primitive mentality.* (French) Translated 1966. Boston: Beacon Press.

LURIA, A. R. 1976. *Cognitive development: its cultural and social foundations.* Cambridge: Harvard University Press.

MALINOWSKI, B. 1922. *Argonauts of the western Pacific.* London: Routledge.

———. 1954. *Magic, science and religion and other essays.* Garden City: Doubleday Anchor Books.

———. 1965. *Coral gardens and their magic.* Vol. 1: *A study of the methods of tilling the soil and of agricultural rites in the Trobriand Islands.* Vol. 2: *The language of magic and gardening.* Bloomington: Indiana

University Press.

METZGER, D., AND G. WILLIAMS. 1963. A formal ethnographic analysis of Tenejapa lading weddings. *American Anthropologist* 65:1076-1101.

———. 1966. Procedures and results in the study of native cognitive systems: Tzeltal firewood. *American Anthropologist* 68:398-407.

MILLER, G. A. 1956. The magical number seven, plus or minus two: some limits on our capacity for processing information. *Psychological Review* 63:81-97.

MILLER, G. A., E. GALANTER, AND K. H. PRIBRAM. 1960. *Plans and the structure of behavior.* New York: Holt, Rinehart, and Winston.

MOERMAN, M. 1969. A little knowledge. In *Cognitive anthropology,* ed. S. Tyler. New York: Holt, Rinehart, and Winston.

NEISSER, U. 1976. *Cognition and reality.* San Francisco: Freeman.

NEWELL, A., AND J. SHAW. 1957. Programming the logic theory machine. Proceedings of the western joint computer conference, pp. 230-240.

NEWELL, A., AND H. A. SIMON. 1972. *Human problem solving.* Englewood Cliffs, N.J.: Prentice-Hall.

PIAGET, J. 1951. *Play, dreams, and imitation in childhood.* New York: Norton.

POLYA, G. 1954. *Patterns of plausible inference.* Princeton: Princeton University Press.

POWELL, H. A. 1956. An analysis of present day social structure in the Trobriands. Ph.D. diss., University of London.

QUINE, W. 1960. *Word and object.* Cambridge: MIT Press.

RAPPAPORT, R. 1968. *Pigs for the ancestors.* New Haven: Yale University Press.

ROSCH, E. 1974. Universals and cultural specifics in human categorization. In *Cross cultural perspectives on learning,* ed. R. Brislin, S. Bochner, and W. Lonner. New York: Halstead Press.

RUMELHART, D. 1975. Notes on a schema for stories. In *Representation and understanding: studies in cognitive science,* ed. D. G. Bobrow and A. M. Collins. New York: Academic Press.

RUMELHART, D. E., P. H. LINDSAY, AND D. A. NORMAN. 1972. A process model for long term memory. In *Organization of memory,* ed. E. Tulving and W. Donaldson. New York: Academic Press.

SCHANK, R. 1972. Conceptual dependency: a theory of natural language understanding. *Cognitive Psychology* 3(4):552-631.

SCHANK, R., AND R. ABELSON. 1977. *Scripts, plans, goals, and understanding.* New York: Academic Press.

TRIANDIS, H. 1972. *The analysis of subjective culture.* New York: John Wiley and Sons.

WALLACE, A. F. C. 1965. The problem of psychological validity of componential analysis. *American Anthropologist* 67(5):229-248.

WASON, P. C., AND P. N. JOHNSON-LAIRD. 1972. *Psychology of reasoning: structure and content.* Cambridge: Harvard University Press.

WEINER, A. B. 1976. *Women of value, men of renown.* Austin: University of Texas Press.

WINOGRAD, T. 1972. *Understanding natural language.* New York: Academic Press.

Glossary

The syntactic markers that denote number in nouns do not attach to the nouns themselves in the Trobriand language but appear instead on the verbs and adjectives. For this reason, there is no simple way to indicate the plural forms of Trobriand nouns which appear in the English texts.

Stress in most Trobriand words falls on the penultimate syllable. The consonants b, d, g, k, l, m, n, p, r, s, t, v, w, y sound much as they do in English. The vowels a, e, i, o, u are sounded as in Spanish. Thus, a as in father; e as in cafe; i as in machine; o as in cove; u as in chute.

baleku: an individually apportioned garden plot when not under cultivation

bilekuvivila: a garden plot held by a woman

dala: local matrilineal descent group

guyau: persons of high-ranking *dala*

gumgweguya: persons of intermediate rank *dala,* below *guyau* but above *tokai*

kaikeda: a gardening arrangement by which a person who has use rights in a garden allows another person to garden it, and receives a portion of the harvest in return

kaivatam: literally, the poles erected next to the yam sprouts, which the growing vines climb upon; metaphorically, the yearly production of yam gardens for another person

kaiyasa: an intravillage gardening competition in which the harvest produce goes to an individual who has organized the event

karewaga: right, responsibility, control; specifically, the right of allocation in the context of garden litigation

kasali: to allocate rights in a resource

kasesila: adjective denoting a resource that has been allocated

katumamata: a payment which "wakes up" a previous *pokala* between *dala,* allowing the use rights in a piece of land to remain outside the owning *dala* after the death of the previous holder of use rights

katuyumali: a payment by which the owning *dala* recovers the use rights in a garden that has gone to another *dala*

keda: road or path; the way of a garden through the social world

kula: a system of periodic exchanges of shell valuables that involves persons throughout the southern Massim area

kumila: the four major exogamous totemic clans into which all of mankind is divided: Malasi, Lukuba, Lukwasisiga, and Lukulabuta

kwabila: a major gardening field; the unit fenced by the gardening community, which may contain more than 100 *baleku*

liku: tall, decorative yam house; the prerogative of persons of power

liliu: the sacred myths upon which original titles in land are based

odila: undomesticated land

pokala: a prestation intended to induce reciprocal exchange

pwaipwaiya: generic land

sagali: a ceremonial distribution of goods

savali: prestations made prior to the declaration of *pokala*

titavana: warmed up left-over food; used as a metaphor for *katumamata* payments

tokai: commoners; persons of low rank

tokarewaga: person with control over a socially significant resource

tolibaleku: the controller of a *baleku*

tolipwaipwaiya: a member of the owning *dala*

toyamata: caretaker; holder of use rights in a garden

tupwa: left over, extra; a garden which has not yet been allocated by its current holder and is thus obtainable through *pokala*

vavagi: generic things

velina: a child's repayment to parent for the work put in by the parent in raising the child

wokosi: the extinction of a *dala*

yakala: public litigation, often, but not necessarily, about land

yolova: payment for health care

Index